Rest in Peace, not Pieces
A 10-Step End-of-Life Planner

J D KING

ISBN 978-1-7395239-0-9 (Paperback)
ISBN 978-1-7395239-1-6 (Ebook)
ISBN 978-1-7395239-3-0 (Hardcover)

Table of Contents

> **Don't Agonize, Organize**
> **– Florynce Kennedy**

Introduction

Are your affairs in order?

No one wants to think about death and dying, but one thing's for sure, we all have an expiration date. Even so, taking the 'I'll deal with it tomorrow' route or pretending that nothing's going to happen for a long time often leaves family and loved ones not only dealing with grief but a literal mess.

It's not morbid to talk to friends and family about what you want when you die. It's something all of us should do sooner rather than later. So many of us put it off, thinking that we'll get to it, and then we never do.

Does your family know what to do with your possessions? Do they know whether or not you have a life insurance policy? What about your finances? Do you have debts and a mortgage? Even more troubling for loved ones is deciding how you are to be buried. Do they know what you want?

Making end-of-life decisions now is actually your final act of love for your family. You have a lifetime of paperwork, accounts and account numbers, passwords, and just a lot of extra stuff that they might not even know about, nor how to deal with. Organizing your life and how you want to leave it can be daunting, but if you take it step-by-step, it's a manageable process. Once it's done, you can rest easier.

Don't try to do everything all at once. The book is broken down into 10 steps. Work your way through methodically. Be systematic and resist the temptation to jump around. Taking small steps is the key to success.

I have also listed various organizations/professional bodies that you may wish to contact to help you in your task. As this book is meant for audiences in the US and UK, you will sometimes see two sets of information and you can choose, depending on where you live, which applies to you.

When you know how to get organized and you've planned for the unexpected, you'll feel better, and so will your loved ones.

How do I know? I've been there.

I'm a married woman with a son in his 20s. I run a business, look after my home and my family, including my own widowed mother who has dementia. My mother was a strong, single parent of three children. She lost her husband when we were small but went on to forge a successful nursing career.

Sadly, she now endures the later stages of Alzheimer's.

It's a common theme that daughters are often expected to take on the responsibility of ageing parents. It may also be the case that little, if any, help will come from siblings or extended family, due to circumstances, distance, and so forth. In my case, I am fully responsible for my mother, who now lives in a care facility near my home. Before she entered a care home though, I spent years looking after her.

My experience made me realize how many of us are simply not prepared. When I needed to take responsibility for my mother, I had to wade through a myriad of challenges: how to manage the money, how to deal with the banks (having a power of attorney is crucial), how to deal with paperwork such as insurance matters and getting my mother's financial obligations put in my name so that I could take care of them. I had to sort through her belongings, all the while dealing with the gradual loss of my mother before she faded away, which, essentially, is what having a parent with dementia is like.

In short, my experiences taught me that there are steps people should take to organize their lives before they die. Being 'tidy' with your life has long-lasting benefits both for you and those you leave behind.

So let's get started.

Step 1:
Communication is Essential

It's alarming to realize that approximately two out of three Americans don't have some kind of end-of-life plan in place.

In the UK, numbers are just as dismal.

Even more disquieting is that a portion of those who say they don't plan on creating one! In fact, roughly 41% of those surveyed said that creating a will or some end-of-life plan would require something like a medical concern or diagnosis.

According to another source, only around 33% of American adults have completed documents pertaining to estate or end-of-life planning, and 60% have stated that they don't plan on doing it. Why? One of the most common excuses is not only the topic itself (many think it's morbid to plan for one's death ahead of time), but that it's too complicated, time-consuming, and expensive.

It really isn't if you take it one step at a time.

Why is making an end-of-life decision now such a big deal? Because you just never know. Therefore, it's important to have plans in place that leave your loved ones with a set of instructions. That way, they can tackle issues involving finances, your taxes, credit card and mortgage companies, and down to the smallest details such as contacting the electric company or your internet provider to notify them to stop billing cycles.

End-of-life planning can be confusing to some, what with trying to figure out the difference between a living will, a living trust, and whether or not an attorney/solicitor is needed. Then there's the perceived difficulties of pre-planning a funeral years before it might ever be needed. Why spend so much time and effort on something that hasn't happened yet?

The simple answer? Your family.

Unfortunately, things happen. Don't let your family be taken off guard. Don't make them worry about your finances or debts, or even how to pay for your funeral (even if you want one).

Don't make them guess how to make the best use of money left in Dad's bank account to pay bills or other expenses. Don't create a situation where family members might disagree about what to do with Mom's car, the furniture and other 'stuff' that's been collected over the years and has to be dealt with before the house is sold or the apartment rented.

Most importantly, don't leave your life without making a will or at least a letter of instruction for those left behind. Why? Because if you don't, they will be left with a number of legal hoops to jump through to either inherit any assets or to deal with any debts left over, the sale of a house or other property, and any number of other issues.

A word about probate and intestacy

If a person dies without a will, any property to heirs will be put on hold based on state laws in a process known as **intestate succession**. Every state in the country has its own statutes or laws regarding this issue. When a person dies without a will, or no instructions are left behind naming beneficiaries, heirs, or how to deal with financial assets or debts, the court decides (based on state law), how remaining assets will be dealt with.

In the UK, laws regarding intestacy depend on the country of origin: England and Wales, Scotland, and Northern Ireland. Only married or civil partners or other close relatives (at the time of death) might inherit based on the rules of intestacy. Divisions of inheritance will depend on the value of the estate. If a civil partnership has been legally ended or a couple has divorced, they typically cannot inherit based on intestacy rules. Also be aware that rules may differ based on situation. Visit gov.uk or Citizens Advice.org.uk for more information about intestacy.

The process known as probate is simply a court procedure that makes determinations on how taxes, debts owed, as well as a deceased person's assets, savings, and so forth are to be organized and distributed. This can take lots of time, and on average, a year.

Be aware that even if you have a will, this probate process will occur, but having a will makes it much easier for the judge and the court to ensure that your instructions are carried out in a timely manner.

It's also important to keep in mind that some US states are shared-debt states, meaning that a surviving spouse may be responsible for the spouse's debts such as credit card debt incurred during the course of a marriage, whether or not that surviving spouse's name is on a credit card or other debt agreement. These states include: Arizona, California, Idaho, Louisiana, Nevada, New Mexico, Texas, Washington, and Wisconsin.

In the UK, a surviving spouse who doesn't have joint finances (mortgage, loans, credit card, or joint bank account) with a deceased spouse is generally not held liable for repayment. A surviving spouse would be responsible only if the agreement or contract is under both names or you were a co-signer. However, surviving spouses are responsible for council taxes if over 18 years of age and you lived on the property at the time the debt arose.

Avoiding family conflict

Family conflicts and disagreements are unfortunately common after the death of a loved one, and even more so when no instruction or will is left behind. Sometimes, issues that exist between family members can explode following the death, especially when it comes to property, money, or even a loved one's belongings. Unfortunately, once an older family member passes away, the 'glue' that held the family together often collapses.

Not having your affairs in order can make such situations even worse.

Without a will, without some kind of instructions for those left behind, the journey of tying up your loose ends and settling affairs can be chaotic, to say the least. Things like probate can prevent the sale of a house for a year or more. Dealing with creditors is aggravating at the least. In fact, how do you even know what a loved one wants in regard to how to dispense savings, stocks/shares, assets, as well as liabilities if you can't even get into their accounts because you don't have their passwords or PIN numbers?

Communication is essential. So what should you do?

Start organizing!

Make your loved ones aware of your end-of-life plans, but before you do that, you have to organize your belongings and put valuable information in one place.

What kind of valuable information? Start a list containing information and documents related to:

- Real estate records that include mortgage. (Whether paid off or not. If the home has been paid off, notify surviving loved ones where title/deeds are located)
- Where your yearly tax returns are kept
- A list of financial accounts including retirement and investments. Make sure that any beneficiaries are updated or confirmed

Important note: When beneficiaries are listed on an account such as a life insurance policy, be aware that the beneficiary named on that account will supersede the beneficiaries in a will (if they are not one and the same). In other words, a person listed as a beneficiary will receive the assets listed even if that beneficiary is not listed in the will.

In the UK, if a person has a life insurance policy and dies without naming a beneficiary (rare), the estate of the deceased typically receives the funds of the life insurance policy which are then distributed according to the wishes of the person's will. The advice of a solicitor can help clarify such issues for those living in the UK.

Also included in your organization strategy:

- A list of personal belongings that you're designating for specific family members. This can include anything from a vehicle to a favorite chair to a treasured book to a valuable piece of jewelry

- Life insurance policy information, account numbers, and contact information
- Online account access information

Not everybody stores their important information online or sends it to the cloud. However, many people of all ages maintain electronic files that can be stored on external hard drives or flash drives. In order to access any of it, you'll need usernames and passwords.

Many of us store those usernames and passwords on our phones. Others write them in a 'little black book', while still others may have them scattered all over the place on bits of paper.

Put all your log-in or usernames and passwords in one place. Have a master copy for yourself and make another one for your executor, your estate attorney/solicitor, or a trusted family member or friend. Make sure to keep this list updated.

Conclusion

Communication with your loved ones is the most important first step in organizing your end-of-life plans. Make sure that your family is aware that you have made such a plan and then ensure that at least one other person has a copy of it. We'll discuss estate attorneys (probate solicitors in the UK), executors and estate planning in an upcoming chapter, but for now, focus on these few basic steps to get you started:

- Start working on organizing your important documents, including a list of accounts, usernames, and passwords (this also includes access to desktop computers, laptop computers, iPads, tablets, and iPhones)
- Make sure someone in your family (or an attorney/solicitor) is made aware of the location of

important documents. These will be explained in more detail in upcoming chapters and can include but are not limited to:

- Letter of intent
- A will or trust
- Who you have designated as a beneficiary or beneficiaries
- Durable/lasting power of attorney
- Medical (healthcare) power of attorney
- Any instructions regarding guardianship (a guardian and a backup guardian for under-age children)

In the UK, a medical or healthcare 'durable power of attorney' is known as a 'lasting power of attorney' or LPA. The lasting power of attorney allows a person to choose someone to act on their behalf when it comes to health and personal welfare issues. However, a separate form is required for those who also need someone to make certain decisions regarding financial and property affairs. You can contact the UK Office of Public Guardian for LPA issues.

Your family and friends are important to you. Remember that they're going to be grieving your loss as it is. Don't add more burden on their shoulders, forcing them to figure out how to deal with your stuff. Remember, that 'stuff' can mean anything from real estate to your family photographs. Include close family members in your end-of-life plans and maintain open lines of communication while doing so.

This way, you will ease the grief of your passing, but also reduce the chances of leaving a mess behind.

At the end of every step, you'll find a Planner Page, which you can use to keep track of your progress.

Rest in Peace, not Pieces

A 10-Step End-of-Life Planner

Step 1: Communication is Essential

Task	In Progress	Done	Location
Start making a will			
Choose some you trust to share your end-of-life plan with			
Find and organize real estate records/rent/ mortgage documents			
Organize your tax returns			
Make a list of financial (bills) accounts			
Make a list of insurance policy info/account numbers/contact info			
Make sure any beneficiaries are updated			
Create a current list of accounts with usernames and passwords			

Additional notes

....

....

....

....

....

....

....

....

....

....

....

....

....

....

....

....

....

....

....

Planner pages available to download here

Step 2:
Passwords and PINs

When was the last time you shared any usernames, passwords, or PINs with a family member, if ever? Do you even have them written down? So many people don't keep a written record of this kind of information, and either keep it in their heads or in their iPhones or tablets.

Even if you do write down user names or passwords, they're often scattered around on a piece of paper somewhere, which is only slightly better than not writing them down at all. If you're like many people, you use different usernames, passwords, and PIN numbers for different accounts, from credit cards to automatic debits, to banking information, and so forth.

Think about it. What is your 'point of digital entry' when it comes to your life, financial records, documents, and so forth? Is it your desktop or laptop computer? An iPhone? A wire-bound notebook? Does anyone in your family know your log-in information to your devices?

This is an important issue to be dealt with, especially due to the prevalence of digital storage utilized these days. However, this consideration can even go beyond online digital vaults (more on those in just a bit).

First, a word about iPhones

If you happen to keep all your log-in information on your iPhone, make sure that a trusted family member can get into it in the event that it is locked. This is vital. What about those phones that can only be unlocked with biometrics such as facial recognition software or a fingerprint scan?

Such a scenario can cause undue stress and intense worry for those left behind. Newspaper articles abound where families are unable to access passcodes or files containing account numbers, usernames, and passwords that must be accessed to take care of financial or legal issues following a person's death.

Any family member charged with dealing with the affairs of a deceased loved one whose life has literally been stored in digital devices, especially for estate planning reasons, must have access before it might be needed.

For this reason, it's advised that such individuals create what is known as a 'digital asset clause' in a will or in a letter of instruction to an executor, estate attorney or trusted family member.

Note to remember: Never put log-in or password information in an official document such as a will or a letter of instruction, as it will become a public document that is filed with the court. This goes for the US and the UK.

Without information on accessing data in a deceased person's phone, the executor, or a family relative *might* request access to a person's iCloud account through a court order, but this takes time and might not be successful.

Be aware that many phone companies, such as Apple, are quite stringent in maintaining account privacy, and unlocking such devices may be impossible. Yes, impossible! Again, per Apple, it is impossible to unlock an iPhone when an account holder dies. They might be able to restore the phone, but only the phone so that it works, but all data stored on the phone will be erased.

What are digital vaults?

Digital vaults are cloud-based options that have become increasingly common for storing important data, including, but not limited to, estate planning documents, wills, account numbers, mortgage information, and so forth.

Digital vaults are not just cloud-based storage areas but are known to offer bank-level security. A digital vault should be secured by strong encryption, such as 256 bit AES, and they should also have a two-part or two-factor authentication process for access. The platform administrators themselves do not have access to the data that is uploaded. Digital vaults are less vulnerable to security breaches than the 'regular' cloud.

Digital vaults are known for their very secure online platforms. People store anything from their usernames and passwords for all of their online accounts, to video and media files, crypto currencies, and more.

Some digital vaults enable you, the user, to control settings as to who will be granted access to the vault in the event of an emergency or a death, such as your power of attorney.

Digital vaults are affordable, with the bulk of platforms available today offering plans with reasonable monthly or yearly payment options. However, it's important to know exactly what the digital vault platform offers, including storage space, the ability to share an account with another user, and the ability to include log-in information for your digital accounts and passwords. Price range may differ depending on the amount of storage space you'll need.

Some of those popular digital vault options available to users today include but are not limited to:

- Lastpass
- Zoho Vault
- Bitwarden
- 1Password
- Dashlane
- Nordpass
- Password Boss
- Keeper Password Manager & Digital Vault
- LogMeOnce Password Management

However, if you don't like or feel comfortable with using a digital vault, you have other options.

Other digital options

Cloud storage, digital vaults, or file folders on your computer or iPhone are not the only options for saving information that you don't particularly want to keep on paper. External hard drives known as passports or flash drives are also an excellent option.

External hard drives are extremely affordable, and most can hold up to 5 TB of information. Popular brands today are also compatible not only with Windows systems, but Mac, PlayStation, and even Xbox devices.

The best part of external hard drives or flash drives is that you don't have to store the information on your computer. You can make one or more copies of your important data on the flash drives. For example, you can have one flash drive that contains all your account information and numbers, as well as usernames and passwords for online log-in.

You might feel uncomfortable giving one person *all* your data – although this should not be the case when you're considering end-of-life decisions and have chosen someone you trust. Whether an executor, an attorney, or an estate planner, make sure you trust that person 100% with your very private and personal financial information. I'm just saying that if you feel better separating the data onto separate flash drives, that is an option – although that might also get a bit complicated, especially if family members or friends you've given such flash drives to move away or, heaven forbid, pass on before you!

It's better that you make one or two copies: give one to a trusted friend or family member and keep another one in *your* files as well.

It's strongly recommended that – if you decide to go the flash drive or external hard drive route – you create files (file folders) on that hard drive or flash drive for separate parts of your valuable information. For example, separate folders for password and PINs, another for investments, one for mortgage or property information, as well as important documents such as insurance policies, house deeds, wills, and so forth. When you open the drive, you'll see all the folders neatly organized so you can make changes or update easily without having to wade through dozens of documents listed with no rhyme or reason.

However, there's one other option for creating a source that contains all your account numbers, usernames, log-ins, passwords, or PIN numbers. It's called a hard copy, or in other words, paper. If you feel more comfortable going old school, that's up to you. Sometimes, going old school is easier and much simpler.

Gather and store important 'hard copy' documents in a safe place

What if you're not super comfortable putting all your private information and important usernames, passwords, and PINs in a digital format? That's okay. Not all of us are tech savvy or feel comfortable about having something 'out there' that we can't see or touch.

Not only that, but in spite of the advantages of technology, it's always a good idea to have a Plan B. For this reason, it's important to always keep a hard copy of account numbers, usernames, and passwords available to an executor, your estate planner, or a trusted family member or friend.

One of the best ways to organize information regarding your documents is to make a master list in a binder, in a 'little black book', or even in a folder with a typed (much easier to read) list that has all your accounts, account numbers, and your log-in access to them. This can be stored in a safety deposit box at your bank or in a locked safe or strong box (also one that is fireproof) stored somewhere in your home.

Of course, you don't want everyone and their brother to know you have a safe hidden beneath the floorboards, but it is important for your surviving family members, your executor, or your attorney to know where it is. Not telling someone is just as bad as locking them out of your iPhone!

This is especially true if you happen to rent a home owned by an individual or rental management company, and the same applies to apartments. In fact, most landlords require basic information about you and who to contact in the event of an emergency. Make sure that you know, through your rental agreement, the process the owner may take in the event of your death. Who will be allowed into the apartment or house to dispose of your belongings? Or, as it happens, to be able to access that safe you might have had installed behind a closet wall or beneath the floorboards? Just something to think about.

Make sure someone you trust, such as your executor, your attorney, or a family member knows where the key is. If you opt for a strong box or portable safe with the key code or combination, make sure someone knows it. Again, use of biometrics may give you peace of mind while you're alive, but it might not work out so great after you're gone, especially for an executor, trusted family member, or your attorney who might have trouble accessing it.

Wrapping up

Now is an excellent time for you to be aware of just how much personal information you have stored in file cabinets, on flash drives, on your computer, or on your iPhone.

Another thing to remember when providing information about your financial matters is to write down not only the business entity, but customer service numbers for that specific company and its address. This will also make dealing with such companies a lot easier later on.

Don't forget that this information isn't just important in order for an executor or a trusted loved one to access your accounts, but to also provide those companies with information such as death certificates. Submission of a death certificate is sometimes the only way to close out an account or to enable an attorney/solicitor or your executor to prove to the company that you are actually gone.

Providing your loved ones or your designated representative with the company name, the customer service number, and even the physical address, can make their job a lot easier. In fact, it may seem morbid and unnecessary, but try to consider one of those 'what happens if...' worst-case scenarios. Cover all the bases you can think of. Try not to leave anything to chance.

Next up? It's time to get into the nitty-gritty when it comes to money matters.

Rest in Peace, not Pieces

A 10-Step End-of-Life Planner

Step 2: Passwords and PINs

Task	In Progress	Done	Location
Create a single source for your account usernames and PIN or passwords			
Make sure you write down your phone passcode for digital devices like your phone or tablet			
Write down your cloud access information			
Check into digital vaults			
Consider flash drives/external hard drive for account information			
Store hard-copy information in a safe place			

Additional notes

....
....
....
....
....
....
....
....
....
....
....
....
....
....
....
....
....
....
....
....
....
....
....

Planner pages available to download here

Step 3:
Money Matters

How on earth do you start getting your financial affairs in order? It can feel daunting, not to mention time-consuming. Everyone has a different way of maintaining their monthly billing and payment systems. Some people take advantage of auto-pay/direct debit while others pay bills online as they come in, while others still write checks.

Each system requires some organization. So whether you're using a good old-fashioned filing cabinet, a simple cardboard box where paid bills get dumped, or you do everything online, the person you have tapped to deal with what you leave behind has to know your system.

Think of it this way. How many bank accounts do you have, including checking, joint accounts, and savings accounts? Do you have stock/share or investment accounts? What about credit card accounts, your utilities accounts, and even your cable or online streaming accounts? While we've been taught to keep our private information private, it can seem to go against the grain to simply write it all down and give it to someone, or have it all written down in one place, can't it?

But in end-of-life planning, this is essential.

In the previous chapter, I emphasized the importance of organizing all those accounts, usernames, passwords, PINs, in one location. But are they organized? Have you forgotten anything?

One of the first steps in organizing your money matters is to make it so that your next of kin, your executor, or a friend who you trust is able to access that information easily, without having to get court orders or deal with emotional tugs-of-war with family members at such a crucial time. It does happen.

Top Tip: While you can, open a joint bank account with your executor. When you die, it will remain open. However, any bank accounts that are in your name only are frozen upon your death, creating unnecessary complications (and a lot of hoops to jump through) for those left behind. The same applies both to the US and the UK. You must be either a joint owner, the estate executor, or a beneficiary of the account. In the US this can be achieved by making sure that you name a 'payable-on-death' (POD) or 'transfer-on-death' (TOD) beneficiary.

The information you need to gather also goes for any stocks, savings accounts, investment accounts, insurance policies, and accounts that might also link to your 401(k)s, pensions, and so forth.

In the UK, a workplace pension or a self-invested personal pension (SIPP) is equivalent to a 401k in the US. However, *state pensions* – paid for by contributing National Insurance payments – can be claimed once state pension age is reached. Refer to gov.uk for guidance.

Remember that it's not only *how much* information you have, but how you *organize* it that is primarily important.

Important note: Don't start this next part until you have completed what you were supposed to have started in Step 2, organizing all your accounts, your usernames, passwords, log-in codes, and information in one place.

If you have not done this yet, Do Not Pass Go, Do Not Collect $200. Get that part finished *before* you move on to the steps in this chapter. If you have done so, give yourself a pat on the back. Now, this next part is another important part of organizing your files and information for those left behind.

This section regarding money matters will focus on not only your bank accounts, but your assets (property, real estate, investments), as well as your liabilities including credit card debt, mortgage, and so forth. It will also include any investments that you have.

When it comes to property, that can mean anything from your furniture to your vehicle, from a boat to a piece of land, or another home property, regardless of where it's located. Last but not least, information regarding any retirement funds and/or pension options.

However, before you even *start* organizing, you need to take the time to create a document that should go in the front of any following information. Think of it as a Table of Contents if you want to. This is called a *personal information document* that can be kept in a master folder, a safety deposit box (that someone has access to!), or in a digital vault. Create one and keep it current. See below for an example of how this could look. This document should contain:

- Your full, legal name (you can include maiden name if applicable)
- Your Social Security/National Insurance number. (You can also include the details of another family member that may have predeceased you, from whom you have been receiving any benefits, including pension payments, and so forth)
- Your legal current residence

- Location and date of your birth
- The full name – and again, Social Security/NI numbers – and addresses of your spouse and children.
- A single source for any birth certificates, marriage certificates, divorce documents, citizenship records, adoption records, and the death certificate of any family member from whom you have been receiving benefits

Another important note: Every US state has a Bureau of Vital Statistics from which an individual can obtain copies of birth certificates, marriage, legal separation, divorce documents, and so forth. (In the UK, such information can be accessed through the General Register Office or locally through your city or town hall Register Office – Office of Births, Deaths, and Marriage.) It will make the search a lot easier if you know the county and city of the individual's birth or death. The same applies to divorce documents, marriage certificates, and separation agreements. You will want to get *certified* copies, which cost a little more, but are more than worth it in the end.

- A list of employers and dates of employment if applicable. You might also want to have information regarding when you first started collecting Social Security, if applicable
- Military records if applicable. This is important for any potential veteran's benefits or insurance policies that are in place for veterans or family members. At the very least, dates of service, military organization, and date of discharge, as well as discharge status (honorable, dishonorable, medical, etc)
- In the UK, don't forget war pensions/compensation schemes per gov.uk

- The name and phone number of any religious entities such as your church and its pastor, priest, or bishop
- Names as well as contact information of relatives, physicians, lawyers, financial advisors, estate planners, and close friends, as applicable

For those in the UK, it's worth telling your relatives about the Tell Us Once service. This is available from the government's Department for Work and Pensions department. It's a downloadable PDF file that notifies government departments and local councils upon someone's death. This includes Her Majesty's Revenue and Customs (HMRC) notifications.

There is also the Death Notification Service created by Equiniti that is available from some banking institutions. It notifies other financial institutions where the deceased held accounts and is a free online service.

Take your time with drawing up the personal information document. It sounds like a lot, but once you get that part organized, you'll have the process down pat and you'll be able to tackle the next part. Again, taking one step at a time will help prevent you from becoming overwhelmed or even *more* disorganized as you continue through this book.

Now it's time to move on to your specific financial information documents.

Your financial information

The next important aspect when it comes to money matters is your financial information. This category should contain information, whether written down on paper or stored on some digital format. When applicable, write down or make a note of how you make payments and the payment due dates (online, by check, auto debit, etc.).

Important financial information to keep organized includes:

- Social Security information
- Any insurance information, along with their business names, companies, agent names, phone numbers, and policy numbers. This includes all-in-one policies or separate policies such as life insurance, home insurance, auto insurance, renter's insurance, umbrella policies, and even long-term care policies
- Information regarding healthcare policies, including Medicare, Medicaid, disability income, and so forth. In the UK, this is private health insurance. Disability income ends after death
- The name of all banks where you have an account, whether it's a credit union, a checking/current account, more than one checking account, savings account, and whether you have CDs or any type of investment, money market, or other accounts at those banks. The same applies to the UK
- Stockbroker information, such as Schwab, Edward Jones, or any other investment income entity. List all your stocks, your bonds, your property, the stockbroker's names, and their contact information. This also applies to the UK, via firms such as BlackRock, Vanguard, JP Morgan, etc
- A copy of your most recent income tax return (you might want to include at least two or three years' worth of your tax records as well, just to be on the safe side).
- Mortgage information. This can also include titles, deeds, and escrow information, anything that pertains to your home. This is especially true for an original deed of trust for your home! Don't forget the

homeowner's insurance policy if you want to keep a copy with the mortgage info

- If you rent, maintain a copy of your most recent lease agreement
- Information regarding car registration and titles. If you owe on your car, include information about the lender. If it's paid for, the title or ownership
- Any property liabilities, including property tax, homeowner's association dues and so forth. In the UK, this is known as a Council Tax on domestic properties, determined by local authorities

Next up in importance is information regarding health, in regard to:

- The location of your most recent will, with your notarized signature and date! Even in the event that your estate planner or attorney has a copy, keep a copy for yourself too
- As mentioned, a list of any credit and/or debit cards.
- Pharmacies where prescriptions are filled
- Physician/GP's name and contact information
- Your medical power of attorney (more on this later)
- Your living will (more on this later)
- A copy of any applicable Do Not Resuscitate or DNR orders. In the UK, this is known as a 'Do Not Attempt Cardiopulmonary Resuscitation', or DNACPR
- A copy of your Advance Directives in the event of a medical emergency. The UK has the 'Advance Decision to Refuse Treatment' or ADRT or a Living Will

- Health information, policy and contact numbers and information

Again, I'll cover these topics regarding health matters in another chapter, along with what they mean and why they're important to have.

All of this financial information and other information is important. Having it all organized and in one place will make it much easier for those you leave behind to take care of.

No one can know exactly when the end will come, but if you plan ahead and act accordingly, you'll leave less to chance.

Now, exactly what are these documents that you need to gather and how can you organize them in a neat and tidy manner that not only you can find easily, but that makes it a lot easier for your executor or loved one to understand?

If it makes it easier, copy down the basic documents listed above, and tackle them one at a time. Remember to utilize the Planner Pages that will make organization and progress easier to track. Place a checkmark or cross them off the to-do list as you proceed. Take breaks and don't rush. You don't have to get all this done in a day!

Organization is the key to success. Take it in pieces. Delegate an hour a day of your time to deal with one or two items at a time. Then take a break. I'm not saying to drag this process out for months, but don't try to do it all in a day or two. If you do, you're likely to miss something or end up with a HUGE mess that can cause you even more frustration.

The next chapter will provide tips and strategies when it comes to gathering and putting your important documents in order.

EXAMPLE OF PERSONAL INFORMATION
DOCUMENT FOR
(YOUR FULL LEGAL NAME)

Information	Numbers/ log-in/ PIN	Contact name/ telephone/ email	Docu- ment Location	Notes
Social Security number				
Legal current address				
Date/place of birth				
Spouse/children full names				
List of employers/ dates of employment				
Social Security info				
Insurance policies				
Healthcare policies				
Bank/invest-ment accounts				
Credit/Debit cards				
Income tax return				
Mortgage: titles deeds, escrow				
Rental lease agreement				

Car reg details				
Property liabilities				
Will				
Prescriptions				
Pharmacies where prescriptions filled				
Physician's details				
Medical Power of Attorney				
Living will				
Copy of DNR				
Advance Directives				
Health Policy Information				

Planner pages available to download here

Rest in Peace, not Pieces
A 10-Step End-of-Life Planner

Step 3: Money Matters

Task	In Progress	Done	Location
Make a list of all your bank accounts			
Make a list stock or investment accounts			
Make a list of monthly bills and account numbers			
Make a list of 401ks or pension fund accounts			
Gather birth and death certificates, passports, marriage or divorce documents			
Create a 'personal information' document			
Gather and organize any military records			
Make a list of attorneys, estate planners, or financial advisors			
Gather any DNR, Advanced Directives			

Additional notes

....
....
....
....
....
....
....
....
....
....
....
....
....
....
....
....
....
....
....
....
....
....

Planner pages available to download here

Step 4:
Organizing Your Documents

This is a long chapter, so don't feel as if you need to read it all at once. You can take it in pieces if it's easier. When it comes to organizing your documents, do that in steps. Some people are more organized than others. I know a friend who is pretty organized and keeps all her bills, home or insurance, along with healthcare bills and summaries in folders in plastic boxes complete with color-coded tabs. She's diligent. Others simply toss everything into a cardboard box and might go through it every once in a while, to find something. Most of us are somewhere in between.

Okay. All I'm saying is don't try to remember everything after a single reading. (Actually, that goes for all the content found in this book – go back and review on a regular basis. This is when those end-of-chapter planners will come in handy!)

The last chapter mentioned the most important documents for you to gather and organize. Where are they now? Do you have them in one file or box or are they here and there and all over the place? Do you have printed copies of what you need or will you have to get them downloaded and saved onto your flash drive or external hard drive? If they're on paper, are the documents in good shape or are they bent and battered, or perhaps stained with coffee spills or in any other way difficult to read?

In the previous chapter I discussed the importance of making a list of accounts, account numbers, log-in usernames, passwords, and PINs. As mentioned, this information is applicable to just about every part of our lives these days.

The same is true of organizing your documents. With today's digital environments, it's important to have access to those documents at the tap of a finger, but it's also important for you – as well as your loved ones or the person you have tapped to be the executor of your will – to know what those documents say. For example, you may have a life insurance policy that you told a loved one about, but are they aware of the stipulations associated with that life insurance policy?

It's understandable that discussing or even preplanning for your demise is uncomfortable, but the more you know about your documents and what each contains, and how those documents can help guide your survivors past your death and settle your affairs as quickly and seamlessly as possible, the more you have the potential to relieve a huge amount of anxiety not only from your shoulders but from theirs.

Tips for gathering your documents

Before you head into this part, it's important to know that *patience is key*. You may realize that you actually don't have a hard copy of an entire life insurance policy, or that you've never saved it in a file folder on your desktop, or even in the cloud or in a digital vault – or that you might end up finding the pages scattered in a box with other loose papers in the back of your closet.

It is suggested that you have at least one hard copy of the most important documents that can be given to a loved one or trusted family friend, or stored in a safety deposit box in your bank. This way, a surviving family member or friend will be able to quickly gain access to important paperwork and be able to thoroughly read through and review the documents and keep them on hand to refer to as needed.

Chances are that even if you have your information stored electronically, your executor or whomever is going to be taking care of your final wishes is going to want a copy. They will need easy access to those documents in order to have information readily available for review with a banking administrator, the funeral home, etc.

This is not a hard and fast rule, so if you don't feel comfortable organizing your documents on paper, that's up to you. Just keep in mind that it might be quite difficult to review an entire will on a small phone screen, and that formatting can widely differ between laptops, iPhones, tablets, and so forth.

That said, you may be wondering: *what exactly* are the most important documents that you need to organize?

Important: If you don't have any documentation started, don't worry. Review the most important ones that will be discussed and then take steps to get them done. Then come back to this chapter and organize as needed.

What documents are the most important?

While most of the documents you have are going to be important, some are simply vital. I'll provide a brief overview of the most common documents you'll need. More details on some of these will be offered in later chapters.

Last Will and Testament

The first important document that you need to address is your Last Will and Testament. This legal document tells your surviving loved ones about any property you have and how you want it disbursed or taken care of. Or, at the other end of the spectrum, obligations (such as debts) that need to be taken care of after your death.

Don't forget that a last will can also specify a guardian for underage children if you happen to pass away before they reach adulthood, or a person who you want to manage your estate after you've died. In most cases, the will is the most important part of estate planning, regardless of how much property you have or don't have.

Durable Financial Power of Attorney

Another important document to have on hand is a **Durable Financial Power of Attorney (POA)** if the situation warrants it. This document gives someone else the power to make financial decisions in the event that you're unable to do so yourself. This type of document is most commonly used to head off chaos or confusion when someone has had an accident and is in a coma, unable to speak, is in end-of-life care, has advanced dementia, and other situations where that person is unable or incapable of making such decisions themselves.

In the UK the document is called a Lasting Power of Attorney or LPA and has two parts: one regards health and welfare matters and the other refers to property and financial matters. As in the US, a lasting power of attorney in the UK does not have to be an actual 'attorney' – it's a matter of following the wishes of the 'patient' or acting in their best interest in case of serious illness.

Remember that until you die, your bills have to get paid. This document enables your financial power of attorney to do important things like file your taxes, pay your bills, and arrange for payment of medical expenses after insurance coverage ends, and so forth.

The 'durable' part of the document means that the person you choose to be your financial power of attorney has the authority to continue acting in that manner in the event that you become permanently (or mentally) unable to make financial decisions.

As an example, many spouses designate the other as their financial power of attorney, especially in cases where one person is primarily responsible for taking care of managing and paying the bills.

Organ donation specifications

Driver's licenses from every US state specify whether you want to be an organ donor in the event you are in an accident and don't survive. In the UK, those who wish to donate their organs must register with the NHS Organ Donor Register. However, in England, all adults are now considered to have agreed to be an organ donor when they die, unless they have recorded a decision not to donate. This is referred to as 'opt out', so you still have a choice of being a donor or not.

Whether or not you choose to be one, your family needs to know your decision. Keep in mind that, in the US, by designating yourself as a donor on your driver's license or state identification card gives the state *legal authority to remove any tissues or body organs upon your death*.

Just in case you're curious, what happens then is that the hospital will review your medical history and determine the viability of any organs following your demise. They will then make contact with organ donor organizations scattered across the country.

In most cases, the possibility of organ donation options are discussed with family members at the hospital. This is the important part. *Always* let your family members know your intentions. After you're gone, some families resist organ donation, even if you've designated yourself as an organ donor on your license. While the majority of family members usually acquiesce with the wishes of their deceased loved ones, don't take chances.

Another option is to obtain an organ donor card that you carry in your purse or wallet. The donor organ card (in the US) specifies which of your tissues or organs you wish to donate, as long as they are viable. This issue can also be taken care of in advanced healthcare directives (discussed in a later chapter) or in a living will.

You can even specify limitations or restrictions for the use of your organs for transplant, such as only for medical research, or for educational purposes.

At any rate, to stave off any disagreements later, put your individual wishes in writing. Make sure that paperwork is included in your end-of-life documents or get the paperwork started while you're organizing your documents.

Additional information on organ donation can be found on the website for the Health Resources and Services Administration at organdonor.gov.

Pet Trust

Let's not forget our four-legged, furry, or feathered loved ones. A Pet Trust is also something to consider if you have pets that are considered true blue members of the family (and they usually are!). While you may have a very different definition of your pet, whether it's a parrot or a cat or a pygmy pig, after you die, those pets are considered property by state law. Don't forget to leave written instructions for the care of your pet or pets in the event you become incapacitated, or you die. While in most cases, a family member or even a friend is more than willing to take on that responsibility, why take the chance?

In the UK, you can also add a **pet** trust to your will or trust. Some pet trusts may pay out in one lump sum for the care of a pet, calculated on age and life expectancy of the pet. Make sure that the pet's name, gender, breed, and age are listed in the trust. Other options such as rehoming your beloved pet can be found via the Dogs Trust organization.

Reminder: In most cases and when it is discussed ahead of time, a family member or friend will often volunteer to care for your pet after you go, but always consider the cost of doing so. Veterinary visits, yearly vaccinations, or an illness, food, bedding, and even toys can be expensive. Whenever possible, have some money put aside for the care of that pet to reduce any hardship on the pet caregiver.

In a pet trust, you can specify who you would designate as a pet caregiver and, if available, even stipulate a sum of money that is to be paid on a regular basis to that caregiver for pet care needs. You can also specify how such monies are to be used and can include anything from medical treatments to purchasing food and toys.

A pet trust is more often engaged in the care of larger animals, such as a horse, or those with very long life spans, or in the event that a pet has special medical needs. For further information on pet trusts, you can access the American Society for the Prevention of Cruelty to Animals and access their pet planning information.

Don't forget to gather any information regarding current pet insurance in your paperwork, as well as the location of your preferred veterinarian! They will also be able to transfer any medical records/history for your pet to a new provider, if needed due to location.

I'll go into more detail about his topic in a later chapter.

Life Insurance Policy

Another very important document to gather together is your **life insurance policy**. Life insurance policies come in a variety of types, and some have stipulations regarding accessing payouts. Some people, especially those who live alone, and who have few surviving family members or friends, may feel that it's not a big deal to not have a life insurance policy.

However, keep in mind that if you don't have an insurance policy when you die, your loved ones may be on the hook for any outstanding debts, funeral costs, and more. In the UK, only the signatories listed on any debt and/or paperwork are liable, but any monies owed are typically taken out of the estate of the deceased.

When you die, your *estate* (everything you own) is distributed as per the wishes of your will, specifying what goes where and who gets what. However, as mentioned earlier, if you don't have a will, your estate will go through probate and it will be the judge who makes the decision as to how any remaining assets are dispersed. In most cases, any assets will first be used to pay any outstanding debts and tax obligations.

Then any money left over will be used to pay creditors or secured debts (including balance on a car loan or even a mortgage) and then whatever is left will be dispersed to the heirs. However, if you don't have enough money to take care of your debts or tax obligations, lenders of any secured debt (again, car loans or mortgages) may repossess other collateral, such as a car or a boat, to sell in order to put toward the debt.

Unsecured debt (including unsecured personal loans or credit card debt) is generally discharged if the estate doesn't have enough money to pay those.

Note to remember: Every US state has their own regulations regarding the repayment of unsecured debt. In most cases, while federal student loans may be discharged, a private student loan may not be – it all depends on the terms of the loan. The same applies to medical debt. In some states, surviving family members may be responsible for repayment, and the same is true with credit card debt. In most states, as mentioned earlier, credit card debt is typically discharged unless you happen to live in one of the nine community property states (Arizona, California, Idaho, Louisiana, Nevada, New Mexico, Texas, Washington, and Wisconsin).

It is recommended, even if it's a small amount, that everyone has a life insurance policy. You don't always have to go to the lawyer to get one. Many insurance companies bundle auto, home, renters, and life insurance into their policies, making it easier than you might imagine to have enough life insurance to pay your debts when you die.

When all is said and done, whether you have a lot of assets or not, having a life insurance policy can provide peace of mind to those you leave behind. While you might not need it, it's always good to have, and even a small life insurance policy is readily affordable for most.

Non-probate Assets Forms

Some assets don't have to go through probate, and payouts can go directly to whomever you specify as a beneficiary. These are called non-probate assets. Maintain a list of these. Some examples of **non-probate assets** in the US include but are not limited to:

- 401(k) beneficiaries
- Pension plan beneficiaries
- Life insurance policy beneficiaries
- Assets that have been specified in a revocable living trust while you are still alive

That said, such assets are taxable.

For those who live in the UK, assets that (typically) don't go through probate include jointly held assets, low value assets (usually under £500 or less), instances of a Discretionary Trust or benefits within certain life assurance policies. Different rules may apply to Scotland and Northern Ireland. Be aware that you may need to contact the deceased person's bank and mortgage company to determine if probate is needed.

Probate may not be needed if the deceased only had a savings account, owned money or shares with someone (which usually goes to the surviving co-owner) or owned land or property as a 'joint tenant', which would also pass to the surviving owner.

Keep in mind that you have to fill out a beneficiary designation form from every one of these entities or providers. These assets, because they are separate, don't need to be listed as assets in your will. Every entity or institution will have its own forms to fill out, so it's best to contact them directly and request downloadable or mail-in forms. Follow their instructions for completion.

Keep copies of these in your documents!

Revocable Living Trust

Another important document that meets the needs of many is called a **revocable living trust**. While it may sound much like a will, a revocable living trust is not. In fact, the revocable living trust is actually a legal property or entity, if you will. In other words, a revocable living trust is allowed to 'own' its own property. With this kind of trust, you can transfer assets to the trust. In order to disseminate assets, you can appoint a trustee, who is able to access as well as manage those properties.

One of the things that make a revocable living trust different from a regular will is that the assets in the revocable living trust don't have to go through probate, which reduces time and streamlines the transfer of assets to designated beneficiaries.

In the UK, revocable living trusts are a legal and binding document. What makes them increasingly popular in the UK is that beneficiaries of such a trust can avoid the probate stage.

There are many kinds of trusts in the UK, as well as trustee tax responsibilities. It is recommended that a consultation with a solicitor can help you wade through the rules and regulations that apply to a number of difference scenarios when it comes to living trusts.

Instructions regarding digital assets

Digital assets and digital vaults and ensuring that a surviving family member or designated individual has access to your digital information was discussed in Step 2. Your designated executor will also need to access this information in order to not only manage those accounts but if required after business is taken care of, to shut down those accounts.

This is especially important for any assets that utilize crypto currencies, or assets that are not treated in the same manner as 'regular' assets such as those you hold in your bank. Be aware that if a private key to access crypto currency assets is lost, misplaced, or unknown by a surviving family member or friend, those assets may be impossible to recover. Always make sure that instructions regarding access are included in your documentation.

Funeral planning

Not everyone expects nor wants a funeral, a memorial service, or even a celebration of life party or get-together. However, such stipulations must be clear for those you leave behind. In fact, if you want a funeral or a memorial, it's highly recommended that you make your own arrangements based on your own desires before you die. Planning ahead not only reduces stress on those left behind but gives them a guideline of what you want and what you don't.

Documents regarding funeral planning or instructions on what to do after you die can include details such as whether you want to be cremated or not. If you do, what do you want done with your ashes? Do you want them placed in an urn or scattered somewhere (some places don't want ashes scattered on their properties. Make sure you know the rules before you designate such a spot, especially in non-rural settings).

Do you want a traditional burial (with coffin) or cremation, or a 'green' burial (no embalming or use of pesticides at the site)?

Some green burials include wood or biodegradable coffins or boxes (cardboard, willow, wicker, etc), or simply being buried in a pine coffin and in a grave that has not been lined with cement or metal. Others may opt for a simple burial shroud. Or you might consider a biodegradable cremation urn.

The choices are nearly endless today, including your remains being buried in a tree pod or even having your cremated remains placed in a floating and dissolvable urn.

Planning your funeral ahead of time also means planning what kind of service you might want, and where you want to be laid to rest. It's growing increasingly common today for individuals to purchase cemetery plots before they die, which again, can make life easier for your loved ones. Some of these details can certainly be included in your will, but to be on the safe side, create a separate document of your wishes following your death in regard to preferences. These instructions can include anything from what clothes you want to be buried or cremated in, to details regarding the dispensation of your remains.

In the UK, choices and decisions for funeral planning are also available. Funeral plans are typically arranged with the guidance of a funeral director, but you don't have to do it that way. If you would prefer to make arrangements without a funeral direction, seek help or guidance through the Natural Death Centre or your local authority's Cemeteries and Crematorium department.

Last but not least

Your end-of-life plan starts with not only gathering documents, but storing them in a place that is accessible to your executor or a trusted friend or family member. I've mentioned a safe, a filing cabinet, or even a safety deposit box, but it's important, no matter which you choose, to let the important people in your life, your executor, or even your attorney-agent, know where those documents are.

It might be hard to talk about end-of-life topics with your loved ones, but it's important to let them know what your wishes are. Doing so may help relieve them of end-of-life burdens that don't need to be on their shoulders. It may also provide them with relief, because they'll know exactly what you want them to do and they won't have to guess and wonder forever if they've done the right thing or if you would have gone along with their decisions regarding end-of-life care.

Important! After you've gathered your documents and put them in order, make sure that you review them occasionally and keep everything up to date. Things change. People move. Sometimes, the person you might've chosen to take care of your affairs will pass away before you do. Children are born, people are divorced, married, or might've moved to a different country!

Never hesitate to contact an attorney/solicitor for a consultation regarding your efforts to organize important documents. Most attorneys offer free consultations that at least can provide you with some guidance. Discuss fees and services with them, especially when finalizing your documents to ensure that you have everything you need.

Next up: Estate planning.

Rest in Peace, not Pieces

A 10-Step End-of-Life Planner

Step 4: Organizing Your Documents

Task	In Progress	Done	Location
Do you already have a will or gotten a life insurance policy? Living Trust?			
Make at least one hard copy of your most important documents (such as will or life insurance policy)			
Have you chosen a durable power of attorney?			
Have you specified if you want to be an organ donor?			
If you have a pet, create a pet trust			
Make a list of non-probate assets			
Start thinking about funeral options			
Don't forget your list of account numbers and PINs for your documents			

Additional notes

....
....
....
....
....
....
....
....
....
....
....
....
....
....
....
....
....
....
....
....
....
....

Planner pages available to download here

Step 5:
Estate Planning

Even saying the words 'estate planning' elicits more than a few groans from many. Comments like *time-consuming*, *complicated*, and *confusing* are common. It doesn't have to be any of those things if you take it one step at a time. If you've been diligent, you're already halfway to completing your end-of-life wishes.

Hopefully, you've communicated with your loved ones about your intention to organize your end-of-life affairs (or improve what you have already done) so that everyone is aware of what you want. You've tackled a plan of attack to organize your account passwords, usernames, passwords, and PINs. You've taken stock of your money matters, your bank accounts, your assets, your investments, your property, and your liabilities.

In the previous chapter, you've learned about the most important ones to complete.

Now you're ready for the next step. If you don't have a will written yet, it's time to do so. In this chapter, I want to explain the different types of wills you can create. A will is not a one-size-fits-all document. You can cater the type of will to your personal needs and wishes. So let's get started.

Different kinds of wills

The **simple will** is a document that specifies who is going to get what after you die. This is often the preferred type of will used by people who don't have a lot of property, money, or investments. In other words, a simple will is common for those who don't have a lot of assets, or who do not expect anyone to challenge the Last Will and Testament, such as a gaggle of relatives.

The **complex will** is commonly preferred by individuals who have more than a few assets, as well as special preferences as far as dividing properties, investments, and so forth. This type of will is also often preferred by individuals who want to leave a certain amount of assets to a family member who has disabilities, has medical needs that must be taken care of over their lifetime, or a friend or family member who is less well-off than others of the family and you want to gift with some money or other assets. This kind of will is also the best kind of vehicle in the creation of a protective trust for a child.

Note for UK: While different types of wills are recognized in the US (as are explained further in this chapter), the UK doesn't have a bunch of 'standard' will types. So, in the UK (rules differ for Scotland and Northern Ireland) anyone can write a will, but if it is not simple or straightforward, it is recommended that you get advice. At its most basic, a will in the UK should decide who benefits from what, who should take care of any children, designate someone to act as your executor, and so forth, just as you would with simple wills in the US.

Legal advice is recommended if you:

- Have property with someone (not a spouse or civil partner).

- Want to leave property or funds for a dependent who is unable to care for themselves
- Anticipate family members who might make a claim on your will
- Your primary residence is outside of the UK
- You own overseas property
- You own a business

Ensure that the will is valid! To write your own will in the UK, you must be over 18 years old and be of 'sound mind'. You must also be able to claim it is voluntary and it should be in writing. It must be signed by **two** witnesses older than 18, and finally, those two witnesses must also sign it, in your presence.

Note: In the UK, you are not allowed to leave witnesses or their partners anything in your will.

Back to the US types of wills…

A **living will** is a type of will that doesn't specifically determine who will inherit what assets or in what amount. In other words, *a living will has nothing to do with the distribution of any property or assets following your death.* It is strictly intended for your wishes regarding medical treatments in the event you become incapacitated. A living will is often confused with advance directives when it comes to medical care.

That said, a living will is often considered a *type* of advanced directive. In its most simplified terms, a living will is a written document that specifies your health care in regard to your preferences for *end-of-life care* in the event of a terminal illness or diagnosis and you are no longer able to make any decisions by yourself (in case you're unconscious, in a coma, or suffering from later stages of dementia, or so forth).

In this case, this kind of living will specifies your preferences in regard to life-support or no life-support, as well as any religious preferences.

Important note: A living will is not to be confused with an advance directive, although they are similar in nature.

An **advance directive** is similar to a living will, although it is not particularly geared to someone who has a terminal illness or is in an advanced stage of illness that takes away the cognitive ability to make decisions for oneself. Advanced directives can be specified by individuals of any age and more often come into play in 'what to do in the event of an accident or severe medical situation' that leaves you unable to specify your wishes. Like a living will, an advance directive also includes situations such as a stroke, a coma, or advanced stages of dementia.

When preparing your documents, be aware that a living will is a specific and separate document. So is designating a Medical Power of Attorney document or a Do Not Resuscitate (DNR) order. I'll discuss more about the specifics of a DNR order and medical power of attorney document in an upcoming chapter but please don't skip ahead! The goal of this book is to take this process step-by-step to help you stay organized, on track, and definitely not overwhelmed!

For now, gather any documents (even if they're just notes scribbled by you) that you have already prepared in regard to your end-of-life wishes. If you don't have them already, it's time to consider doing that.

When it comes to estate planning, one of the primary reasons people put it off is because it's expensive. In most cases it can cost anywhere from $1000-$3000 or more to create even a basic estate plan package.

The Testamentary Trust will

There is also what is known as a **testamentary trust will**. This type of will is typically used for bequeathing monies or assets to any family members who are under a certain age. In many cases, such beneficiaries won't receive their inheritance until they reach their early 20s, and sometimes well into their 30s, depending on circumstances and the wishes you stipulate in the will.

This kind of will involves anyone who wants to put some of their assets into a trust that will benefit an heir or survivor that may not be of legal age yet. For example, you can put money in a trust and put any type of condition on inheritance as you wish, including age or other stipulations, such as only being dispersed after college is finished, or being dispersed when certain conditions have been met by the heir.

This type of will does undergo the probate process. In addition, the terms of a testamentary trust cannot be changed or revoked after you die. This prevents the trustee from making any changes that you might not have agreed to.

Joint will

Another type of will is known as a joint will. In this case, two people (testators) – commonly a married couple or siblings – can create a shared estate plan. Like the testamentary trust, joint wills cannot change when one of the testators passes away. Neither can the executors, beneficiaries, nor other stipulations of the will.

Because of the strictures against making any changes after the death of a spouse or partner, based on changing circumstances or so forth, this type of will is not as common as each spouse making their own will. In the event of partnerships that may not be recognized officially by the state, the probate process can be more complicated.

There are several other types of wills as well, including what is known as a **deathbed will**. This type of will is spontaneous and may occur when someone is dying, considered spontaneous in nature. A spoken or written statement can refer to a deathbed will. If such is the case, witnesses are highly recommended.

However, because of circumstances and the mental state of the dying individual, deathbed wills can conflict with other prearranged documentation or even contain mistakes or confusion regarding intentions. Therefore, deathbed wills have a greater chance of being contested or challenged in court. In some circumstances, because of the uncertainty of the 'of sound mind' recommendation for those making wills, they might be dropped in court altogether, especially when it is believed that important information or contradicting information is found in it.

Making your own will

You don't have to go through an estate planning attorney or a lawyer to create a will and last testament. You can do it yourself. A number of options for downloading standard forms are readily available. A number of online and end-of-life forms and death planning kits are available for download. They can cost much less, ranging from absolutely free to several hundred dollars, depending on what you need.

However, you must ensure that the will *follows the laws of your state in regard to the viability of that will.* You must also understand the probate laws of your county and state, as all wills, as mentioned earlier, will go through probate court.

For example, some states honor handwritten wills (known as holographic wills), but be aware that specific requirements must be met. Those requirements include:

- Your own signature. Be aware that in some states, like Idaho, if you can't write the will and its provisions in your own hand, and then sign it, then your hand-written will may not be valid
- Having the will witnessed and notarized. Again, state requirements differ on self-proofing that the will is legitimate and legal
- Be careful not to hamper the ability of the person you choose to be your executor or your personal representative to be able to access the 'informal version of probate' that will enable that person to avoid the courtroom process

Again, a handwritten will is more easily challenged than one that is prepared by a legal representative so take this approach with extreme caution. Before considering creation of a handwritten will, no matter how simple it is, you will need to verify the specific laws in your state and county to ensure that the document is viable. At the least, it is always recommended that after you've written a holographic or handwritten will that an attorney reviews it for accuracy.

A lot of this may sound confusing, but take it one step at a time. You can have more than one kind of will in place, such as having a living will and a simple will. Why? Because they serve totally different purposes. In the event that you do feel that you need more than one will for your estate planning needs, it's always best to also consult an attorney to make sure that the wills coincide with one another and don't contain conflicting wishes or information.

Last but not least, make sure that anyone you have designated as your power of attorney is still your designated power of attorney, especially if he or she has moved or has experienced a change in life circumstances that may interfere with their ability to perform their duties with due diligence.

Here's a recap: A **will** determines (by you) how your estate (in other words, your assets, money, or property) will be distributed to survivors or entities. The **durable power of attorney for finances** designates a person to make financial decisions in the event you are unable to do so. A **living trust** specifies and instructs an individual (the trustee) to hang onto and distribute any funds or properties on your behalf when you can't manage them yourself.

Next up, it's time to Plan your Funeral.

Step 5: Estate Planning

Task	In Progress	Done	Location
If you don't have one yet, decide what type of will you want/need			
Contact an estate planning attorney about questions regarding wills or end-of-life forms based on your state!			
Make your own will – make sure state law is followed!			

Additional notes

....
....
....
....
....
....
....
....
....
....
....
....
....
....
....
....
....
....
....
....
....

Planner pages available to download here

I told you I was ill
– Spike Milligan (carved on his gravestone)

Step 6:
It's Your Funeral

You make careful plans and decisions most of your life, so why not do the same with your funeral? There are a number of benefits to planning your own funeral, memorial service, or celebration of life, or making the decision whether to have a religious or non-religious ceremony. Most importantly, it's up to you!

Knowing the difference between a viewing and visitation, the traditional funeral, a scattering, or other types of funeral or end-of-life send-off is important when considering planning your own. It's not often that you likely think of your own funeral, memorial service, or whether you want one, but as they say, knowledge is power. So too is planning ahead.

Do you know the difference between numerous funeral service options? I've listed 10 of the most common here:

- Visitation
- Viewing
- Wake
- Memorial service
- Funeral service
- Direct burial
- Direct cremation
- Scattering ceremony

67

- Funeral service
- Celebration of life

Let's say you decide to be cremated. Sounds simple enough, doesn't it? But are those services pre-arranged? If they're not, does your family know what to do with your ashes? Do you want them scattered in a particular location, do you want to be placed in an urn and then tucked into a niche at the local cemetery, or do you want your ashes buried?

See? Even a simple decision as telling your loved ones that you want to be cremated isn't enough. It's in the details.

The same applies to burial plans. So now it's time to figure out how you want to leave this world. Do you want to be cremated or buried? Would you like a memorial service? Do you want a religious service, or would you prefer a non-religious ceremony?

These are the kinds of questions that you need to ask yourself. It's also important to know the difference between some of the above-mentioned options.

What's the difference between a viewing and a visitation? Many people often confuse the two, thinking that it means the same thing. A **viewing** involves the presentation of your body in a casket, or in a stiff and well-constructed cardboard box (commonly used in pre-cremation scenarios). Viewings are typically held a day or two before the funeral service at a funeral home.

Note: A viewing is not a term that involves *watching* a cremation. That process is known as 'witnessing' a cremation.

A **visitation** is a gathering that takes place either in a home or a funeral home where the body of the deceased is not present. In other words, it's primarily a term used by those who are 'visiting' with the family of the deceased, a place for friends to gather and to reminisce. It can be rather informal in nature.

However, in the UK, a visitation is often used interchangeably with the 'viewing' and most often refers to a brief ceremony prior to the funeral – the casket is present and family and friends gather to say goodbye.

What's the difference between a funeral service and a memorial service?

Many people interchangeably use the term funeral service or memorial service following the death of a loved one, but they're not the same thing either. The **funeral servic**e is a service that is conducted with the body present, such as in a casket or urn.

A **memorial service** is conducted without the body being present, although an urn containing ashes or a portrait is often set up in plain view of the attendees. In the UK, such services imply a gathering (without the remains of the deceased present) in a church, home, or community hall where speeches, eulogies, quiet contemplation, or music may be played, such as with a celebration of life gathering.

Burial or cremation?

The decision regarding burial or cremation is a very personal one. Some people make that decision based on their religious beliefs. Others base the decision primarily on costs.

Let's start with burial options, in no particular order.

First, a word about direct burials or direct cremations. What are they? They are quite frankly, the quickest and easiest way to be buried or cremated. This type of burial option is quick. Costs are often much lower than traditional funeral or cremation services that include viewing, visitations, and memorials or formal services.

Direct cremation and **direct burial** are also known as 'simple cremation' or 'simple burial'. There is no memorial service involved. For example, if you opt for a direct cremation, a funeral home is notified upon your death. Or they will pick up your body from the location of your death and deliver it directly to a crematorium. Such services are also available in the UK.

After the cremation, someone you choose can come to collect your ashes. In such cases, the facility takes care of important paperwork including death certificates and permits. The same is true of a direct burial. In the UK, check with providers regarding such ancillary services.

Such services are often cheaper because there is no embalming or cosmetic options, which are often requested prior to a viewing. In the event you opt for a direct cremation, you can make adequate arrangements with the crematorium yourself. You don't need a funeral director, which can save money. The staff at the crematorium will take care of required arrangements and paperwork, including the aforementioned death certificates.

If you're not aware of any providers in your area, you can contact the Cremation Association of North America. There are over 400 crematories within that association throughout the country. In the UK, the Co-Op (coop.co.uk) can provide local expertise and advice.

There are cases where your local funeral home will have a crematorium on their premises, although in most cases, funeral homes contract with third parties, so only the cost of transporting the body from the funeral home to the crematorium may be required.

In many cases, if you're opting for burial of your ashes, chances are you might want a traditional funeral service. Such services often start with a viewing, otherwise known as a wake in some regions. In others, this part is left out, especially if you don't opt for an open casket funeral.

Of course, options for urns are up to you in the event you want to be cremated. In some cases, a simple cardboard box or bag filled with the ashes are chosen, as the ashes will soon be scattered anyway. Otherwise, cremation boxes, wooden urns, or ceramic urns will come in different sizes and costs.

A brief mention of other options for burial. In order to save money, to reduce the financial burden on loved ones, or simply because a person may not have any remaining friends, family, or loved ones that are close, donating your body to science is another option. In this kind of scenario, you can offer anything from donating your body to a teaching hospital or for scientific research. I've even known someone who not so jokingly suggested a 'body farm' where stages of decay are observed for the furtherance of forensic and crime scene investigations.

A direct burial is much like the direct cremation. It's a process of burying the deceased as soon as possible, with no funeral beforehand. In other words, burial will occur as soon as possible following death. This is also an option for those who aren't religious or those who don't have any close relatives or friends they want to burden with such obligations.

Before making a decision for a direct burial or cremation, discuss it with friends, family, and loved ones. While this is your choice to make, it might not be a popular one with others who feel that you deserve more. However, families and friends can always opt to hold a memorial service following the direct burial instead of beforehand.

In other words, it's up to you. For many, it comes down to simplicity as well as cost.

In the UK, an 'essential' funeral is a lower-cost option that offers basic funeral services, though some restrictions may apply. Another option is a 'tailored' funeral, which as the name implies, can be catered to the wishes of the deceased or the family in regard to what is or what is not included.

Traditional funeral services

During a traditional funeral service, the religious leader (pastor, priest, minister, rabbi) will offer a short speech or sermon. A eulogy is also given during the funeral service, which is typically offered by a family member or friend to honor the life lived by the deceased. Traditional funerals often include hymns and prayers, but others can include a favorite song or two of the deceased.

After the funeral service, the coffin or remains of the deceased is transported to a local cemetery, followed by a funeral procession of family and guests to the burial location. Afterward, family and guests remain for the committal service, or the time during which the coffin or urn is lowered into the grave as your final resting place.

In some cases, people often opt for a simple committal service or graveside service. This is less formal than a traditional funeral process.

In the event of a cremation, family, friends, and loved ones will often gather at the funeral home where the earthly remains of the deceased are kept until the funeral service, and again, may include a procession to the cemetery and the witnessed interment.

Something to consider: Memorial services or funeral services can also be conducted before or after cremation. It's up to you.

Things to consider when planning a traditional funeral

If you opt for a traditional funeral ceremony and you want to make plans ahead of time, make sure to specify everything you want. What kind of clothes do you want to wear in your casket? Be specific. You can write down anything from a well-worn pair of jeans and a favorite T-shirt to a specific dress or suit, or anything in between.

I know someone who wanted her husband of many years cremated in his favorite pair of sweatpants and hooded sweatshirt. After all, he wore them nearly every day and was very comfortable in them.

Would you want a family member to put you in a dress if you never wore one? What about makeup and how you want your hair? Again, it's the little details that make all the difference. It is also these details that take the questions, the uncertainty, and the worries from your loved ones.

When planning your own funeral, it is also highly recommended that you also choose your own casket or method of burial. This will also facilitate the pre-planning stages and reduce any decisions that your loved ones have to make.

Costs come into play when it comes to choosing caskets, flowers, or even a program, reception, and finally, the plot in which you will be buried, or the choice of a memorial urn that will be returned to your family with your ashes.

This is *your* decision! Plenty of people today are eschewing the expenditure of thousands of dollars on a fancy casket that's only going to be seen once before it's lowered into the ground. Make sure that your wishes are known.

Pre-purchasing a plot

Whether you want to be buried in a casket or have your ashes buried in a cemetery plot, this decision is also often based not only on cost, but preferences. When it comes to ashes, you have an option between private mausoleums and community mausoleums, indoors, or outdoors.

When it comes to burial, you have options between private cemeteries on private property, public cemeteries, or a national or state cemetery.

In the UK, cemeteries are generally owned by local authorities or churches. Prior to burials, the family will be required to notify the local registry office in order to receive the necessary documents for the funeral. A certificate enabling a burial is known as a 'green form'. This does not imply a 'green' eco-friendly burial – however, these are also available in the UK!

A word about 'natural' burials

A natural burial is also known as a green burial. These often include the person being buried in a shroud, a biodegradable casket, or other non-toxic materials. In such cases, the embalming process is skipped, or eco-friendly embalming fluid is used. Many cemeteries today have set aside an area that is only for natural or green burials.

The option for natural or green burials are growing by leaps and bounds. Eco-friendly options are enticing to some, such as the use of biodegradable burial containers for ashes, or biodegradable coffins or other direct-to-earth burial of cremated remains or bodies. A few options include wicker coffins, shrouding boards or simple shrouds. If you want to opt for something like this, let the funeral director know and they can obtain what is needed if they don't have any at their location. However, always obtain cost estimates in advance and be aware that the soil conditions in your area must be optimal for biodegradability.

What about scattering ashes?

In the event that you've chosen a relatively traditional funeral service but want your ashes scattered, the funeral home will give your family or loved ones the cremains at the appropriate time, and they take them home.

In some cases, family and friends might want to have a scattering service where friends and family can partake in the scattering of ashes, whether as participants or bystanders. In other cases, scattering of ashes is a very private affair.

Know the laws of the state when it comes to scattering of ashes

Refer to the laws in your state regarding the scattering of ashes. For example, in the state of Wisconsin, there are no laws that restrict a person from scattering ashes in their backyard or on any other owned property. However, if you want to scatter ashes on *someone else's property*, you have to get their permission.

In the event that you wish to have your ashes scattered on water, such as a lake in Wisconsin, federal law requires that it's at least three nautical miles from shore. Also be aware that (in Wisconsin), the Environmental Protection Agency needs to be notified within 30 days of a water burial.

Ashes may also be scattered in cemetery scattering gardens or memorial parks, and if it's on public land, take the time to check with city as well as county offices to ensure that there are no restrictions. What about federal land, such as a national park? Each national park has their own rules regarding the scattering of ashes. To be on the safe side, contact the National Park Service or the park ranger's office that oversees the property and ask about rules or regulations.

In the state of Colorado, each city or county can specify their own regulations regarding the scattering of ashes, as do national parks. Search their websites for information, or give them a call. Like Wisconsin, Colorado allows the scattering of ashes on your own private property or getting permission from another property owner.

When it comes to federal lands in Colorado, while it is recommended to seek permission, scattering of ashes is acceptable as long as ashes are kept away from trails or roads or waterways. Colorado does provide downloadable applications for permits to scatter ashes within some of its parks, such as Colorado's Rocky Mountain National Park.

In the UK, you may also spread ashes anywhere on your own property. If it's not your property, you need permission from landowners – or other relevant authorities if the location belongs to an entity such as the National Trust or national or famous heritage sites. Common sense applies. For example, no permanent markers, no environmental damage or contamination of water sources. Please scatter ashes as discreetly or as privately as possible and in a way that does not interfere with wildlife or the general public.

Celebrations of Life

Celebrations of life have become increasingly popular over the past couple of decades. There is no single way to define such a ceremony because it can be unique to every family. Sometimes, the celebration of life is substituted for a traditional funeral service, but it doesn't have to occur at any specific time. For example, a celebration of life can occur within days of a death, or even weeks or months later. In most cases, the remains are not present at this celebration.

Celebrations of life are typically happier celebrations – and it can include anything you want at your own party such as music, type of food, dancing, and so forth.

So, what exactly do you need to know when it comes to pre-planning your own funeral?

Steps for pre-planning your own funeral

Step #1: Start by making a general list of what you want. This is simply the starting point of your preferences and ideas. This will not be the official document but simply jotting down your thoughts about how you want your own funeral or memorial to go. Also do this even if you don't want a funeral, memorial, or a celebration of life. Whether you live alone and have no nearby or close family members, or a gaggle of them, pre-planning your own funeral makes sense and can reduce conflict, financial strain, and other worries from the shoulders of family and friends.

Step #2: Contact a funeral service provider or funeral home in your area or in the area you wish to be buried. They can help you make decisions and hone any details as needed. Most funeral homes around the country offer free funeral pre-planning services. Many also offer payment plans for you to pre-pay for funeral costs, which simplifies everything for those you leave behind.

Step #3: While the decision of what kind of funeral or burial or service you want is up to you, it's always important to take into consideration your family. Talk to them ahead of time about your intentions. However, it's also important to keep in mind that they're going to need a way in which to honor, remember, as well as grieve your loss.

Step #4: Develop a more precise and detailed written plan or document that spells out exactly what you want. After all, if it's not written down, no one will know what you want. Once you have this document or plan in hand, you can take it back to the funeral home and get an estimate on final costs as well as any options for payment plans.

Step #5: As mentioned, pre-planning your funeral, regardless of what kind it is, is one of the best ways to take a huge burden off the shoulders of your loved ones. That also includes costs. Covering funeral costs ahead of time releases the responsibility for your family to come up with the amount of money needed to cover such costs, especially when a death is unexpected.

Yes, life insurance is available, but there are often delays in payment. Because of this, it is strongly encouraged that you pay for your funeral or burial in advance. Funeral homes do offer funding options, whether it's a payment plan or a one lump sum payment.

Step #6: Once you have settled the arrangements, it's important to let your family and most especially, your emergency contacts, know about your plans. At least two emergency contact persons should know about this, as well as your executor or other close family members. In fact, everyone can have a copy of your funeral services plan, just to cover all your bases.

Your funeral plans should be contained in your important documents. In addition, it is again strongly recommended that close family members also have a copy of your wishes, or you speak to them regarding them. This also avoids family disagreements about what you want. Remember, after a death, emotions are all over the place. Nerves are frayed and grief can either bring out the best or the worst in us.

Conclusion

Pre-planning your own funeral is your decision, but always consider family and friends. While it is ultimately your own choice, sharing your intentions allows others to get used to the idea if you opt for something that's not traditional.

Funerals are expensive, but if you've pre-planned and taken care of costs ahead of time, families and loved ones will be relieved of that financial as well as emotional burden. The same is true for opting for other forms of burial or cremation. Relieving the burden on those remaining are the primary consideration when people make such decisions.

Pre-planning your funeral decisions and options as well as details may be one of the most important aspects of this book, but so too is the next step, regarding medical matters.

Rest in Peace, not Pieces

A 10-Step End-of-Life Planner

Step 6: It's Your Funeral

Task	In Progress	Done	Location
Discuss funeral options with family/friends			
Decide what you want in regard to funeral options			
Start exploring options for burial or cremation			
Start planning your funeral if you want a service, include all the details			
If you decide to be buried, look into options for pre-paying for a burial plot			
If you want to be cremated, look into laws of the state for scattering/burial of ashes			

Additional notes

....
....
....
....
....
....
....
....
....
....
....
....
....
....
....
....
....
....
....
....
....

Planner pages available to download here

Step 7:
Medical Matters

Getting your medical affairs in order is another important aspect of organizing your life before you die. Many of us are guilty of putting off this subject, and unfortunately, by the time it's needed, it's often too late.

When it comes to your medical issues or wishes, get it all down on paper or in an easily accessible digital file. I mentioned some of these medical documents in an earlier chapter. Now let's get into the medical matters in a little more detail here.

Where to start?

First, carefully review this chapter before you do anything. Just absorb the content and then you can go back and determine your own wishes. Don't let the options confuse you. I'm just providing you with information about a number of documents that may be useful to you in your end-of-life planning. Take your time reviewing information about these documents and understanding them and their limitations. Discuss with your doctor before making decisions, and then let your family members and loved ones know what you are intending in regard to your medical matters.

That said, the first thing you need to do is get your doctors' details written down: doctor's name, location, contact information, medical insurance and accounts. That includes your Medicare or Medicaid or Disability and so forth. You are allowed access to your medical records. You can request any information that you want, but if you want printed records, you will have to pay for them. While a lot of people today take advantage of the online portals with their healthcare providers, having this information on paper is also recommended, especially when it comes to current medical issues.

In the UK, citizens are covered by NHS medical care, but many people also have private health insurance. Make sure all information, such as your NHS number, private health details and passwords are kept up to date.

The same applies to your medications.

I talked about the potential for organ donations in an earlier chapter, and you should already have documentation or a written statement regarding this matter in your documents file, but it's also suggested that your doctor have a copy of it as well in your patient medical records.

Now it's time to get into the nitty-gritty of end-of-life care in regard to Do-Not-Resuscitate or DNR documents.

UK residents can take care of such 'advance decision' preferences (commonly also known as a *living will*) at any time, but keep it up to date in regard to preferences. Keep in mind that this is only used in the event you lose the ability to communicate your own decisions regarding treatment.

DNR documents

As I mentioned in the earlier chapter, there are a number of different types of Do-Not-Resuscitate orders. A Do-Not-Resuscitate order (or its equivalent in the UK: DNACPR or 'do not attempt CPR) should be included in your Advance Directives (or can be a separate document) in those end-of-life plans that advise that cardiopulmonary resuscitation (CPR) is not to be administered if you don't wish it. This document is intended for emergency medical personnel, nurses, doctors, and emergency room staff in the event your heart stops or you stop breathing.

Remember! The DNR order only applies to the rendering of CPR and *not* other treatments.

Anyone over 18 years of age has the legal right to have a DNR order in place, as long as you are well and lucid enough to make that decision and to consent to a DNR either in writing or verbally. You need to have one of these documents in your files, as well as one in your medical records.

It's also a good idea to have a copy of your advance directives attached to the refrigerator in your home, which is a common place for first responders to look when responding to any calls for help, especially for older individuals.

DNR orders are typically recommended for someone if they are:

- Incapacitated or in a coma
- Terminally ill
- Any attempts at prolonging life would be futile
- Would create a more difficult medical condition or burden on others based on the expected outcome of the attempted CPR. (For example, if a loved one is suffering from the end stages of a terminal illness, or the individual has a very low chance of recovery either physically or mentally in regard to brain function)

In addition, be aware that there are two primary types of DNR orders – one for non-hospital situations, and another for hospital situations.

The **hospital DNR** is a document that is binding if you are in a nursing home or hospital and have a written or verbal DNR in place. If you haven't had a chance to create a written DNR order, verbal consent can also be given as long as it is witnessed by two adults, and one of those must be a doctor in the admitting facility. Written DNR orders should be witnessed by two adults.

Hospital DNR orders will stay in place while you are in the nursing home or in a hospital, but upon discharge or relocation may expire. Be aware of status or any changes to ensure that they remain in place, especially in the case of long-term care or nursing home facilities.

A **non-hospital DNR** is a document that is typically in the home, often the case when someone is discharged from a nursing home or hospital. This type of document may also be recommended if you are under hospice or palliative care in home-based scenarios. The non-hospital DNR order does not expire, but based on your state, must be renewed every 90 days by your primary physician.

Be aware that in the event you are relocated to another facility and the DNR order has expired, you or your power of medical attorney, loved one, or executor can request, per your wishes, that the DNR order be reinstated.

Remember: The hospital DNR order is *not* applicable to home-based scenarios. A non-hospital DNR order can be approved and issued by your primary care physician for you to have at home. In such a case, if you have an event at home and a family member or friend calls 911, they can be directed to the DNR order and they will not try to resuscitate you or transport you to an emergency room for CPR.

Can you change your mind about a DNR order? Yes! All you have to do is let your doctor know and the order can be removed.

Refer to your county and state DNR resuscitation forms. They will contain information and boxes for you to check regarding resuscitation efforts for hospital transfer, medical workups, antibiotics, and so forth. Most states have downloadable Do-Not-Resuscitate order forms that provide instruction regarding resuscitation in the event of respiratory or cardiac arrest. These forms can also be obtained from your physician or upon entering the hospital.

In addition to the hospital DNR or the non-hospital DNR form, doctors around the country are also using a *medical orders for life-sustaining treatment* form as well as a DNR order.

DNR orders can also include a Do-Not-Intubate order (DNI) which means that you don't want to be put on a ventilator. DNR orders can also include a Do-Not-Hospitalize (DNH) order, stating that you don't want to be sent to hospice facility or hospital for end-of-life treatment or care.

To aid you in getting your affairs in order, an advance care planning infographic in PDF file is downloadable from the National Institute on Aging (NIH).

Medical Orders for Life-Sustaining Treatment (MOLST) document

Medical orders for life-sustaining treatment is a document (again, check your county and state for specifics) that provides end-of-life care planning that includes not only your wishes, but your doctor's judgment depending on the results of medical evaluations.

This kind of document is typically intended for those with an advanced or terminal illness, as well as those who need long-term care services and may die within 12 to 24 months. It can also be put into place for anyone who wants to avoid life-sustaining treatments. It's a little more involved than a simple DNR order and contains information regarding overall health status, care goals, prognosis, as well as the risks and benefits of different kinds of life-sustaining treatment.

The MOLST document cannot be changed without the patient's consent, or the consent of their medical power of attorney or healthcare decision maker. It is not required, but the document must be contained within your files, your medical record, and even kept on your person when you leave home or even in the event of traveling back and forth between care providers! At that time, this document becomes what is known as a portable medical order or **portable orders for life-sustaining treatment**/POLST. Make sure your family and your physicians are aware of this document.

This document is also applicable to EMS service providers. The document has a number of boxes to check under different sections including:

- Resuscitation instructions when the patient has no pulse and/or is not breathing
- Orders for life-sustaining treatment when the patient has a pulse and is breathing

This document also has other treatment guidelines or orders for life-sustaining treatment that include use or delivery of:

- Antibiotics
- Artificially administered fluids and/or nutrition feeding tube

- IVs
- Dialysis

Ask your doctor about these forms and carefully discuss your options with your primary care provider as well as family. In this way, everyone will be on the same page.

The POLST (P for 'portable') document, in its simplest terms, is a way of communicating what you want in regard to medical orders in a variety of scenarios. In some states, this is also known as a Transportable Physicians Orders for Patient Preferences or TPOPP (T for 'transportable') but essentially is the same document.

For example, if you have a medical emergency in the home, you – or your advanced directives – can inform the EMTs whether you want to stay at home or be transported to the hospital. You or a loved one has an option of telling them that you want or do not want them to attempt CPR. It also defines the medical treatments that you want or will allow.

The POLST is typically recommended for those who are extremely frail or terminally ill and provides more details and instructions regarding any future healthcare treatments over and above advanced directives or simple DNR orders.

Contact your physician or your county health department for more information about these documents and legal parameters in your state.

Advanced directives

As mentioned in earlier chapter, advance directives are one of the most important documents in your arsenal when it comes to end-of-life planning. In addition to agreeing to or accepting CPR (cardiopulmonary resuscitation) your advanced directives can also provide detailed information on *what kind* of interventions or life-sustaining care you will accept.

Every state provides forms for advance care planning. You can access state-by-state advance directive forms from the American Association of Retired Persons or AARP or your physician. Forms from different states require careful reading and review. These documents are not to be rushed through, and every aspect of them must be carefully considered. You can discuss certain aspects of these directives with your physician for more detailed information.

For example, the form from Ohio requires signature for special instructions such as, '*I specifically authorize my agent to refuse, or if treatment has started, to withdraw consent to, the provision of artificially or technologically supplied nutrition and hydration if I am in a permanently unconscious state and my physician and at least one other physician who has examined me have determined, to a reasonable degree of medical certainty, that artificially or technologically supplied nutrition and hydration will not provide comfort to me or relieve my pain.*'

The same state also provides special instructions in regard to a person in a terminal condition. For example, '*...if I am in a terminal condition and unable to make my own healthcare decisions, or if I am in a permanently unconscious state and there is no reasonable possibility that I will regain the capacity to make informed decisions, then I direct my physician to let me die naturally, providing me only with comfort care.*'

In other words, when preparing your advanced directives, you have the choice of what you want or don't want, such as tube feeding, IV fluids, antibiotics, insulin, and so forth. You can specify limitations to how long you will remain on life support systems such as ventilators.

Your advanced directives will specify when actions may be taken to postpone death or whether you simply want to be made comfortable with palliative care and pain relief. Most advanced directives also offer adequate space for any additional limitations and/or instructions.

Advanced directive considerations

Your advanced directive considerations must be carefully considered by you and discussed with your family and loved ones, but remember, these are your preferences. In some cases, family members may balk at the limitations you have put on your end-of-life care, but gently remind them, if needed, that your provisions are yours to make.

Careful preparation of your advanced directives and end-of-life wishes will ensure that you get the care that you want and takes away the burden of making decisions from your loved ones.

Remember that advance directives not only include DNR orders or other medical care preferences but must also specify your durable medical power of attorney or attorney for healthcare that can act as your proxy if needed.

Advance care planning is especially important for individuals diagnosed with a terminal illness or for those diagnosed with any form of dementia including Alzheimer's disease, which are terminal conditions.

If you don't have advance care plans and documents in place, decisions regarding your life may be made on your behalf by your physician. Determine the laws of your state by contacting your local county or state legal aid office or the State Bar Association.

That said, be aware that advance directives are recognized legally, but they are not legally binding. Healthcare professionals will always do the best they can to follow and respect your wishes, but depending on the situation, especially in the event of a complex or emergency medical situation, it may be immediately unclear what you want. This is why it's important for you to have this document given to a close friend or loved one and should be included in your medical chart by your physician.

Digital healthcare portals are shared between physicians regularly, and your advanced directives and DNR wishes should be included. Make sure they are! Also, let family members know what you intend, and provide them with copies of such documents as needed.

Conclusion

While you want to take your time with your advanced planning and medical matters and organization, don't put it off. Go through it bit by bit. While you're waiting for additional information or consultation with your physician or family members before you fill out the documents, you can move on to simpler matters when it comes to your end-of-life care and making sure that things are organized before you die.

Rest in Peace, not Pieces
A 10-Step End-of-Life Planner

Step 7: Medical Matters

Task	In Progress	Done	Location
Have you considered your options for end-of-life care?			
Make a list of your doctors, prescriptions, or other medical supplies			
Gather information regarding your healthcare financing (Medicare/Medicaid/Health insurance/Disability) and put with documents			
Create a hospital and non-hospital DNR docs if wanted			
Designate a medical power of attorney			
Create Advance Directive and life-sustaining treatments wanted or not			
Discuss MOLST/POLST with your physician			
Talk to family about your wishes			
Make copies of wishes for family members or friends			
Keep documents updated if changes are made			

Additional notes

....
....
....
....
....
....
....
....
....
....
....
....
....
....
....
....
....
....
....
....
....

Planner pages available to download here

> **Out of clutter find simplicity**
> **– Albert Einstein**

Step 8:
The Stuff of Life

Take a moment to look around your home, regardless of whether it's a large multi-bedroom structure with basement and attic or a one-bedroom apartment. What do you see? Furniture, mementos, memories, as well as practical items. How in the world do you go about dealing with all that before you die? This is especially true for someone who has no children, or extended family members who either live close by or on the other side of the country.

Don't forget that other 'stuff' that makes up part of your life. You might have a vehicle or two, a boat, or even some off-road toys that are covered now more than they used to be. You might have a garage full of tools that are rarely used anymore. What about that massive collection of magazines or baseball cards, or coins that you or a loved one has collected for decades and are now kept in a closet?

Organizing your life before you die doesn't just involve your finances. It involves all that other *stuff* that makes your life enjoyable to you – but that might not mean so much to those you leave behind.

I know an older woman who spent her life with her military husband, who had been deployed all over the world. They collected wonderful pieces of fine china dishware, furniture, and other items from each of those countries they lived in, so much so that they had to rent a small storage shed to store it in. They hoped to pass all those wonderful things down to their children – the lamps, the silver-plated silverware, the tapestries, the carpets and rugs, only to learn that the children, grown now, weren't interested in any of it.

It's important to face reality when it comes to this part of pre-death organization. The plain truth of the matter is that your children, your nieces, or nephews, or maybe even your own brothers and sisters have no desire to inherit your stuff. While it might mean the world to you, it might not mean anything to those you leave behind.

Of course, a memento or two, a keepsake, a family heirloom, those are different. If there's something in particular that one of your family members has often admired, you can certainly bequeath it to them in your will.

First things first.

Take stock and 'gird your loins'

It can be intimidating to start a process of going through those closets, the attic, the cupboards, and even the basement, not to mention a storage shed or two, along with the main rooms of a house or apartment. How do you approach dealing with all that stuff? Take your time with this part, as it is likely to go slower than you expected, especially when you start tripping down memory lane. It's a bittersweet process, one filled with smiles, joy, and love, but it can also be filled with sadness, heartache, and for some, bitterness.

As they say, this part of the process requires that you gird your loins or pull up your bootstraps. You've already come a long way, so don't falter now.

When it comes to deciding who gets what or if anyone gets anything, it's important for you to decide what stays and what goes. Are there some things that could go to charity, to your local church, or to the local Boys or Girls Club?

There are things that you may want to give away before you go, such as special pieces of jewelry or a treasured family heirloom. But as we all know, we all have closets filled with things that have been stored for years. Sometimes, they've been there so long that we don't even remember what's in them!

I've known more than one family who lost a loved one, only to be faced with a house full of stuff that they didn't know what to do with. There was so much of it, from furniture to old letters, to knickknacks, just about everything that most of us save over the years but don't really realize how much of it there is until we have to move. Or die.

You have options. In addition to leaving some treasured items to family, there are a number of other beneficiaries that may benefit from your generosity when it comes to belongings and that 'stuff of life'.

Charities

Local charities are more than happy to receive donations of clothes, toys, some furniture items, books, and anything that might be useful in a household. Such charities include not only Goodwill, but the Salvation Army, AmVets, church charities, and so forth that can be found throughout your town, city, or county. In the UK, you'll find numerous charities that include the British Heart Foundation, Oxfam, Action Change, and more. Many of these charities offer free pick-up services. Some items need to be dropped off at their donation centers.

Not all local charities accept furniture, however, so always call and ask first. Others, like Habitat for Humanity, Salvation Army, and some Goodwill stores will pick up furniture, but again, call first. Obviously, donated furniture should be in good condition.

Vehicles

Other assets can also be gifted to charities, including vehicles. This can include anything from a car to a boat, to RVs, and so forth. Most states have vehicle donation programs, and they are easy to access online. Once you access their website, you might be asked to fill out an online donation form. One of the most popular charities for vehicle or used car donations goes to veterans, some of them for disabled adults. Vehicles for Veterans is just one such charity. In the UK, you can donate a vehicle to any registered charity, but first, make sure they have a UK registered charity number.

Other charities that may appreciate a used vehicle include the Ronald McDonald House. Ronald McDonald houses are usually located near a children's hospital. Family members can stay there for free when a child is in the hospital and the family lives too far away to make the drive every day, or the family might not have a vehicle at all, which is where your donation can come in handy, allowing them easier travel than bus or Uber to get to the hospital.

The UK also has Ronald McDonald House charities throughout the country. Contact them for information regarding car donations, which may help with family transportation at various locations. Or, you may 'scrap' your car and donate the proceeds to the House charity of your choice.

Habitat for Humanity is another charity that often takes vehicles. Vehicles can either be sold or recycled for fundraising purposes.

Pre-arranging home goods donations

For home-based donations, take the time to go through your home, one room at a time, and start organizing. You don't have to give anything away right now, but you can pick out the things you *do* want to donate to such organizations and make a list for your executor or your loved ones so that they know what goes where.

When taking this approach, specify the organizations, the addresses, and the contact information for those donations, such as those listed above. Do everything you can to make dealing with your stuff as easy on your loved ones or executor as possible.

You don't *have* to start cleaning out your house or your apartment right now (though you can start now to make things easier) but organize what you have. It's not a bad idea to go through your things on a regular basis anyway. It's amazing how much we manage to accumulate in just a year!

So make a list of what you DO want to donate and to whom.

One of the easiest ways to approach such a task is to use a wire bound notebook or journal of some sort. If you have a specific piece of jewelry that you want to leave a loved one, specify what it is and who it's going to. You might even take a picture of it and glue it in the notebook so there is no mistaking exactly what is going where. Of course, this is just one idea of how you can keep track of your progress, as well as designating those special belongings to someone you admire and love.

A number of social services in our communities in every state around the country can also take meaningful bequests of belongings, including things that you haven't used in years. There are always those in need, so as long as it's in good condition, there's no such thing as 'Oh, it's too small or too little, no one will want this'. Homeless shelters, battered women's shelters, those providing for foster children, and even refugees often need things.

It's time for spring cleaning!

There's no law that says spring cleaning has to be done in the spring. This is a process that can be started any season. When trying to downsize the stuff in our lives, it's often easier to start with one room at a time. Don't feel as if you have to rush through this process. It can be emotional but it can also be cathartic. A common suggestion is to start with things that have been stuffed into basements or attics, or even those boxes that have been crammed into the garage forever and that you haven't gotten into in years.

This is especially important if you're considering downsizing. However, as cautioned, don't go through all your stuff like gangbusters. It's important to give yourself enough time to deal with what you're doing (and why) along with the cascade of emotions that you may go through in the process. It can be a roller coaster ride for some. Thoughts of guilt, regret, and other negative emotions can make the process difficult. However, keep in mind that just because you let something go doesn't mean that you're also letting those memories or experiences go along with it.

Finally, realize that change is hard, whether you're doing this yourself or for an elderly loved one. To make the job a little bit easier, try not to tackle too much in a single day. I'll reiterate. This kind of spring cleaning takes time. Some decisions may be harder to make than others. Don't pressure yourself or your loved ones, as that only leads to tears and frustration. Finally, remember that it's not just the emotions that must be dealt with, but the physical aspect of the job too.

How do you get started?

To get started, make a list of which rooms you'll be going through first. Divide the objects in each room into categories, as applicable. For example:

- Clothing
- Books
- Furniture
- Sentimental items
- Non-sentimental items
- Create a 'maybe' pile

Don't feel that you need a box for every category. If it's easier, simply make a list or, if you have help, sticking post-its on specific items might also help to streamline the process.

When it comes to downsizing or decluttering or dealing with the things you've collected during a lifetime, it can be hard to get rid of anything. You've grown comfortable with them. Even if you don't see it, just knowing that you have them tucked safely down in the basement or up in the attic can be comforting to many.

Note: Downsizing or going through your life's stuff is often recommended for anyone over the age of 50.

Moving on.

When it comes to organizing and letting go of some of it, you might want to start with things that don't have any particular emotional attachment to them. This would be the easiest part – and this approach can also help you maintain momentum throughout the process.

Next, when going through items, determine which ones are replaceable and which are not. This can also help making the decision a little easier.

About that 'maybe' pile

Be prepared when going from room to room that there may be some things that you can't make a decision on immediately. Put a sticker on those items or write down a list of those 'maybe' items. Keep moving forward. Later, go back to them. Do you *really* want to hang on to those particular items? If you do, keep them. If you're still uncertain, it's a good indication that you don't.

What about the nicer stuff?

If you were a collector in the past (or still are) – whether it be school lunch boxes, baseball cards, *Life* magazines, or signed photos or antiques, or anything else – ask yourself whether hanging onto those things is worthwhile. What if there's no one in your family that would appreciate your collection? Some things that used to be quite valuable or interesting are not so popular anymore. Even when it comes to historical things, such as magazines or that collection of baseball cards, or the newspaper that was saved for the moon landing or other historical events, such things don't always mean as much to younger generations today as they used to.

You don't just want to give those away, but you might consider putting them up for auction, either on websites such as eBay, or if it's a collectible, through an auction house. Not only can this put some extra money in *your* pocket, but you know that that item or set of items will be going to someone who truly wants and appreciates them.

Note to remember: Before you start going through your stuff, let your family know what you're doing and what your intentions are. Don't take it the wrong way if one of them says, 'Oh, I would love to have that' or, 'No thanks.' Do your best not to be offended if something you've treasured for decades is not wanted. You are the one who treasured it. You're the one who gained joy and pleasure from it. Yes, it's hard to let some things go but remember, we can't take it with us.

Keeping the process moving smoothly

When going through your things it's also important to not lose steam in the middle of the job. Again, give yourself adequate time to go through one room at a time, but don't dawdle in the middle of the process. You can rest in between rooms. Give yourself time. When it comes to designating items to family members who need to pick something up or to collect a box or two, give them a deadline. If they really want it, they'll make arrangements to pick it up before that deadline, and if not, it goes to a charity or to someone else.

Setting dates

While it's been repeatedly mentioned that you may not necessarily want to rush through this process of decluttering that stuff of life that you've collected over the years, it's also important not to drag it on endlessly either. Mark a calendar and give yourself an end date for going through every room. If you don't quite meet the target, that's okay, but at least you'll know that you've made some progress.

A few weeks to a month (depending on the size of your home and how much you've collected over the years) is a good window for going through all that stuff. However, also take into consideration age and physical capability when going through this organization process.

Decluttering your life can be extremely difficult for some, but cathartic and relieving for others. Everyone reacts differently to those favorites of life, so don't expect children, friends, or even spouses, to be on the same page as you when it comes to what you save and what you don't. The key is simply to start organizing.

Also keep in mind that decluttering, organizing, or getting rid of stuff that's not being used or hasn't even been seen in a while can make it much easier to move around the living space as well as to clean it. Decluttering will make home maintenance easier, especially for those who are dealing with an illness or a declining physical or mental condition.

So, as a recap, follow these tips:

- Give yourself enough time to do what needs to be done without encouraging the 'I have plenty of time, I'll worry about it tomorrow' attitude, or rushing through things, which can contribute to biting off more than you can chew – which in turn can lead to a sense of emotional and physical exhaustion

- Whenever possible, take emotions out of the process. Choose items that you would want to go to other family members. If they don't want it, it's okay. Get rid of the things that have no emotional attachment or value to you first, and then the rest will be a little bit easier

- Consider giving your loved ones or family members some of the things that you would've bequeathed now, rather than waiting until you've said the final goodbye

Next up, it's time to tackle another difficult topic – wondering what's going to happen to those you leave behind.

Rest in Peace, not Pieces

A 10-Step End-of-Life Planner

Step 8: The Stuff of Life

Task	In Progress	Done	Location
Categorize your 'stuff'			
Tag items you want to give to a family member or friend			
Contact charities in your area about donations			
Pre-arrange for donation pick-up dates			
Declutter each room of the home			
Create a 'maybe' pile			
Contact appraisers for collectibles			
Set a pick-up date for family to pick up things			

Additional notes

....
....
....
....
....
....
....
....
....
....
....
....
....
....
....
....
....
....
....
....
....

Planner pages available to download here

> **We make a living by what we get;**
> **we make a life by what we give**
> **– Winston Churchill**

Step 9:
Arrangements for Loved Ones
Left Behind

Making arrangements for loved ones left behind comes with a huge variety of possible scenarios. However, I'll only be covering the basics for a couple. There's a lot of information to absorb, so don't think you have to remember all of it at once. Take your time (but not too much!). This aspect of getting your affairs in order is vital if you have someone in your life that you *know* you'll worry about if you don't attempt to make plans for them ahead of time.

Who's taking care of whom?

A very close friend of mine, in her mid-60s but in good health and still working, has a handicapped daughter. Ensuring that her daughter is taken care of in the event of her death is one of her primary concerns. What do you do when you have minor children or a disabled child who is also an adult?

Who's going to care for your beloved dog or cat after you die? I talked briefly about the need to designate a friend, family member or loved one to care for a pet in the event of an accident, hospitalization, or even death.

Making arrangements for loved ones left behind takes some careful consideration, especially when someone is sick or disabled, regardless of the diagnosis or prognosis. How in the world do you start to do this?

You've come a long way when it comes to organizing your life before you die, but there are a couple of additional topics that must be addressed, no matter how uncomfortable. One of those is making sure that anyone who needs care, whether it be a child, a handicapped adult, or an elderly relative, continues to be looked after in the event of an incapacitating injury, illness, or if you die.

Yes, that's blunt, but it's also an extremely important topic and one that should not be put off. This is especially important when dealing with a loved one who has developmental disabilities, a child under 18 years of age, or even a family member you've been taking care of who has a terminal illness or is dealing with a form of dementia.

I mentioned earlier in this book that I provided care for my mother, who was diagnosed with dementia. In the beginning, I was only concerned about her welfare and what I could do for her to make her life easier. It was only when the dust settled a bit that I realized that I also needed to make arrangements in the event that something happened to *me*. Who would take care of her then?

Not every scenario can be covered when it comes to making arrangements for loved ones you might leave behind. However, take the time and make the effort. There are numerous options you might choose, and I'll mention a few to get you started.

Note! When reviewing this chapter, remember that you don't have to make any decisions regarding the information found below *immediately*. The information is simply to provide a broad overview of what kind of options you may have when it comes to minor children or dependents, or if you are responsible for someone's care. In the event that you feel a guardianship is required, consult an estate planning attorney/solicitor, who will be able to guide and advise you in greater detail.

First, it's important to define the difference between guardianship and conservatorship. In the UK, this is known as a 'deputyship'. In such cases, this is done by order of the Court of Protection or CoP on behalf of the patient or individual. Two types of deputyship in the UK are the *property and financial affairs* deputy, and the *personal welfare* deputy, regarding medical treatment. All deputies are monitored and held accountable to the Office of the Public Guardian or OPG.

At its most basic definition, a **guardian** is often appointed to oversee the daily needs and care of a minor or ward. There is also an option between legal guardianship and temporary guardianship.

A **conservatorship** is more often one that oversees the legal matters and finances of an incapacitated adult. However, definitions differ between states. There is also a limited conservatorship of the person (personal needs) and the limited conservatorship of the estate (financial needs).

Remember: Such issues should be discussed during the estate planning process as you proceed, as requirements may differ from state to state.

In both cases, a court-appointed individual is designated as a guardian. A family member or a complete stranger can be deemed the guardian. Again, conservatorships primarily focus on financial decisions, and often include the elderly, the mentally disabled, the incapacitated, or those who are unable to make rational financial decisions.

The guardian is typically focused on meeting the personal and health-related needs and decisions of minors under their care.

Thinking ahead

Of course, it's impossible to plan ahead for everything, but it's also a good idea to plan ahead for those 'just in case' scenarios. While it's hard enough making end-of-life decisions for yourself, it can be especially difficult to make them for elderly loved ones or a disabled minor or adult child. That's why planning ahead is so important – and the purpose of this book! It's not just about organizing your life before you die, but thinking of those that you might be leaving behind if something happened to you.

As I mentioned earlier, we all have an expiration date. Organization and end-of-life planning is all about maintaining power. Making decisions based on those 'what if' scenarios is one of the best things that you can do for those you leave behind.

The fewer questions left to surviving family members, the better. I have a friend who is the daughter of a divorced couple. Her parents were estranged and lived in opposite ends of the country. Her father kept his deteriorating health history to himself, but once in a while he did comment that '*if I die, sell the house and contact my investment provider*'. That was it. It sounded fairly simple, but what his two adult children were left with was a mess. While they were able to receive benefits from the investment company as listed beneficiaries, they were still stuck with selling the house, which of course, went into probate because no will had been left behind. It took over a year before the courts were satisfied that the children could inherit the house and then put it up for sale. The process also cost thousands of dollars, and also caused mental and emotional stress that wouldn't have been necessary if their father had organized his life and made a will or a living trust.

Let's explore the topic in more depth. Really, it's important to know.

Guardianship

Guardianship is a legal term that generally defines a situation where a person is appointed by a court to make decisions as needed for someone who is a minor. A variety of scenarios can implement guardianship status. What exactly is it? What does guardianship of a person actually mean? It means that the guardian is taking responsibility for the management of daily and possibly long-term care of that person.

That responsibility includes providing a safe living arrangement, making medical decisions, providing daily care or oversight, and ensuring that basic quality of life needs are available, within possible limitations of such services and resources. A guardian would also be responsible for:

- Deciding where the person will live
- Managing personal property, transportation needs, and ensuring adequate clothing and groceries

Guardianship implies a unique yet legal relationship between two people that is either created by or approved by the court. For example, a guardian can be someone you know, such as a relative, someone you've grown up with, or a long-time friend. In most cases, guardians are chosen from within the family to care for a loved one, such as a child, in the event of the unexpected death of a parent.

Guardians can also be aunts and uncles, grandparents, or even a good family friend. In such cases, a guardian is given legal authority to make decisions for the person under their care (known as a ward) who can't make such decisions for themselves. However, guardianship is often used as a last resort. Alternatives and options are available, as discussed in earlier chapters.

In the below descriptions, you might think that the durable power of attorney wouldn't apply to the care of a minor child, but this power often comes in very handy when it comes to paying for the services rendered to a minor child or a handicapped adult who is unable to make such decisions on their own. This also applies to paying for the care of such an individual in a long-term care setting, a group home, or a nursing home (all of which, by the way, are terribly expensive!)

Guardianship in the UK is known as a 'special guardianship' and also comes with specific stipulations and rules. A person 18 years of age or older can apply for special guardianship if a minor is unable to live with birth parents or have not been legally adopted. This type of guardianship enables a person to make decisions for the minor, from where they go to school to potential medical treatments and decisions. A number of rules apply and in some cases, a person must request permission from a family court to apply. In many cases, such a person is already the child's legal guardian or lives with the guardian through a child arrangement order made by the court. The length of time the child has been in a person's care may also impact rulings. For more information on special guardianship, visit gov.uk for additional details.

Two of the most important alternatives include:

Durable power of attorney (or LPA in the UK) for general and financial issues – such powers can include:

- Buying and selling securities
- Receiving dividends and interest from shares of stocks, bonds, or other investments
- Voting in shareholder meetings
- Investing
- Management and leasing of property – includes sale of real estate
- Acquiring property – such as a vehicle
- Access to digital accounts and assets
- Ensuring ongoing payments for health, life, or property insurance
- Tax obligations
- Access to safety deposit box/s
- Acting as representative with Social Security Administration
- Maintaining oversight of health insurance, including Medicare/Medicaid, Disability accounts

There are more powers that a durable power of attorney can utilize than listed above, so again, consulting with an estate planning attorney is recommended to ensure clear understanding of the rights and obligations of guardians as well as your options when it comes to planning for the care of a dependent in the event something happens to you.

Durable power of attorney for healthcare – a legal document will provide detailed information such as:

- Limitations regarding mental health treatment
- Admissions to a nursing home or community-based residential community

- Statement of desires or limitations for care

Other options include instructions found in documents such as:

- Trusts
- Living wills
- Advanced directives

Guardians are often appointed in the event of the death of a parent and the child or children are under 18 years of age, but guardianship may also be needed in other scenarios involving adults, such as:

- A person needing care due to an incapacitating injury, disability, mental illness, or disease process and that person needs someone to look after their healthcare and living needs
- A person who is unable, mentally or physically, to take care of financial issues, manage themselves, or is unable to make money decisions, or to make medical decisions for their care

However, it's important to note that an injury, mental illness, a disease, or developmental disability is not enough on its own to declare a person incapacitated. As mentioned, guardianship, or conservatorship as it is also called, is primarily limited to minor children in the event that no close, living relatives are able to provide for those children.

In the event that other options have not, or are not, sufficient for certain circumstances, guardianships are vital in protecting vulnerable children or adults. If a child had no one to provide care for him or her, that child may become a ward of the state. In most cases, a child or an adult who becomes a ward of the state has been diagnosed with cognitive difficulties.

Multiple *types* of guardianships can be granted, including:

- Guardian of state
- Guardian of person
- Special guardianship of a person of limited capacity
- Guardian of person and estate

The type of guardianship will be determined by the range of assistance or support that a person may need. Guardianship can be temporary, used in emergency circumstances, and doesn't have to be permanent. Co-guardianships are also an option.

A temporary guardianship is just as the title implies. It is most often used in emergency or critical situations where the property or the individual themselves may be in danger. Temporary guardianship typically has an end date and there are limitations on the powers of the guardian during that time, such as only those that are necessary to address the specific situation or emergency.

In most cases guardianship is used as a last resort depending on the competency or incompetency or limited capacity of the person who might require a guardian.

As mentioned, in most cases, family members or close friend are often chosen as guardians in such circumstances, although professional (non-family) guardians, or those who have received special training, can serve as guardians. Keep in mind that private professional guardians are required to be certified and licensed.

How do you go about designating guardianship? The brief overview described here is for informational purposes only. If you feel the need for a guardianship, consult with your family attorney or an estate planner for more information and details.

Some of the processes involved in designating a guardianship include but are not limited to filing a *general petition for guardianship*. Once it is filed in the court, a hearing date is set. A variety of notices and legal documents will be required (including physician's certificate and assessments) before the hearing. After review, a final order will be given where guardianship is officially declared. In most cases, the official document will be issued by the relevant County Clerk's office. Then, the order of guardianship will be entered into the court system.

If you are considering appointing a guardian for a minor or disabled or elderly loved one, discuss such intentions with your family. By law, a number of people will receive a legal notification of such guardianship proceedings, including spouses, grandparents, and siblings. In regard to legal or professional entities, care facilities and hospitals will also receive notice of guardianship proceedings, as will the Veteran's Administration (for veterans only), and anyone who has been designated as a successor trustee for those who have been significantly involved in the ward's life.

Other types of guardianship are also broken down into specific types, such as:

- Pets
- Financial
- Of the elderly
- For adults
- Of minors
- Medical

Guardianship can be granted as a full guardianship, limited guardianship, or joint guardianship. As the terms specify, a full guardianship gives complete decision-making abilities, authority, and responsibility to one person. A limited guardianship contains limitations, such as focusing on healthcare or property management. A joint guardianship implies more than a single guardian.

Now that those basics are out-of-the-way, let's focus on how you go about choosing a legal guardian.

Things to consider when choosing a legal guardian

Remember that simply by choosing a legal guardian and putting those wishes into your will doesn't mean that you immediately lose control of your child, your elderly mother, or that favorite uncle of yours. You're making plans *ahead of time* and such desires and arrangements are designated in your will or a living will, or advanced directives, depending on the situation. You will maintain control over your dependent/s while you are alive.

Like other aspects of your Last Will and Testament, it's important to make your wishes known. Making sure that any stipulations regarding guardianship or conservatorship are included in your documents, and as always, discuss scenarios and intentions with your loved ones.

How do you go about choosing a legal guardian? The decision is not only a practical one, but one that is likely to be filled with emotions. After all, this is your loved one! You want to choose someone who will provide your loved one with things that you find most important including love, stability, and responsible guidance.

In many cases, adults choose a family member to be a guardian to their child or an elderly or otherwise disabled person in the family for whom you have been caring. Extended family members and friends can also be a good option.

Take certain aspects of those individuals into consideration when narrowing down your choices. Evaluate them based on honest discussions. For example:

- Does the person you're considering want to be a guardian? This is a huge obligation that may affect the guardian's life as much as it affects the ward

- Is that person financially capable of supporting your child or loved one?

- Are they healthy?

- Where do they live? Would your child have to move to a different county or state? Would your child have to go to a different school or make new friends?

- Are they capable of providing your loved one with everything they need to ensure quality of life?

- When choosing someone, try to imagine your child living with this person or people. What do you think their life would be like, and how different from how they live now?

- Does the person you're considering already have a family? Would an addition to that family be resented or put an extra financial burden on them? How many children are currently in that family?

- When you choose a person, especially if they're married, you also have to consider who exactly will be raising your loved one. Let's say you picked your best friend to be your child's guardian. Yet what if she gets married later on and her new husband's not too keen on the idea? What if they're happily married, but their living circumstances change and your best friend has to go to work. Will the child be left in the husband's care or have to spend their days in a childcare facility after school?

Carefully consider not only the best-case scenarios, but the worst-case scenarios when it comes to choosing a guardian. Try to anticipate issues or problems that might crop up. Most importantly, it's vital that you discuss the situation with that person several times.

A lot of people might feel honored to be asked to be the guardian of a minor in the event of your unexpected death, but it also requires careful and thoughtful consideration for everyone involved. This is especially true for non-temporary guardianship or conservatorship scenarios.

I know a woman whose sister asked her to be the guardian to her disabled adult child, who at the time lived in a community-based group home. Later, her child was placed in a nursing home. It's a complicated situation. It was very difficult for the sister to decline, but she did, based on the fact that she was not confident that she would remain in the area forever. She also had adult children of her own, so there was always that 'what if I want to move' scenario.

Others may simply not want the responsibility. Some might have financial difficulties. Some might not be capable of caring for someone even if they're the nicest people in the world.

It's important not to be angry with someone who declines the responsibility of caring for a child or an elderly person. It is much harder than many people think, and many are just not mentally, physically or emotionally prepared to take on that role.

That's why it's very important to take your time making your choice. You might even want to touch base with them every few months to make sure that they are still agreeable.

It's always wise to prepare for the unexpected. You don't have to be old, sick, or elderly to appoint a legal guardian. Such decisions can be made as you're filling out your healthcare directives. Of course, have a Plan B in mind in the event that the person you had hoped would become the guardian has a change of life circumstances, such as an illness or even their own death.

What are the steps involved in appointing a legal guardian?

While it's important to have legal representation when doing so, understanding the basic steps for appointing a legal guardian is included here to provide a broad overview of the process. After all, the more you know, the more specific questions or issues you should be able to ask or address.

Step #1: Determine what type of guardianship is needed.

Step #2: After careful consideration, choose a designated guardian, which can be for your children or other dependents or individuals who rely on you for care.

Step #3: Let other family members know about your decision. If you still have a spouse, you need to be on the same page and agree to the decision.

Step #4: Before finalizing anything, schedule additional discussions with the person or people you would like to serve as guardians, regardless of type. Make sure that they're on the same page in regard to wishes and the maintenance of lifestyle as much as possible of minors, elderly or disabled loved ones. Remember, situations and attitudes change. If you have doubts or concerns, don't hesitate to bring them up with your prospective choice. These are discussions that *must* happen.

Step #5: When it comes to actually setting up the guardianship, you have a number of options. You can include it in your estate planning discussions with an attorney. You can also find appropriate online forms, as well as legal aid offices that you can refer to. However, anyone you talk to *must* be experienced in guardianship and trusts so that in the end, your documents are legally binding and guarantee (as much as life can guarantee anything) that your wishes will be followed.

Step #6: Documents for guardianship must be signed in the presence of witnesses and notarized. Every state has mandates for the number as well as the type of witnesses that are eligible to sign the documentation.

Guardianship should only be used as a last resort, as it does take away a person's individual rights and ability to make decisions. Again, that's why I mentioned other options earlier, such as advanced directives or advance planning, financial powers of attorney, and a living trust.

For additional information regarding guardianship, you can refer to the United States Department of Justice in regards to guardianship.

A few more words about pet guardianship

In an earlier chapter, I briefly mentioned pet guardianship, but this topic requires a bit more detail when it comes to information, options, and considerations than just giving your pet away to an old friend or family member.

For many of us, especially those who are older, a pet is a true blue, down-to-earth member of the family. For real. I'm talking about those people who not only have pets for companionship, but those that truly envelop their pets into the family. They *are* family. For many, a pet is their only companion, and the relationship between the two is one of the strongest bonds one finds in life.

A number of situations may be triggered after you pass away, so it's very important for you to plan in advance regarding the wellbeing of your pets. This part of the chapter specifically focuses on cats and dogs, but I know that there are people who have especially close and loving relationships with their birds or even a barn animal or two. I've known people who've kept pet pygmy pigs that are like their house pets, with their own pig beds and food bowls. I knew an older man who did the same for a swan that he had saved when she was still a cygnet. I know a woman who loved two hedgehogs who pretty much had the run of the house. Shall we talk pygmy goats? Squirrel monkeys? Potbellied pigs? Iguanas, snakes, and lizards…

Regardless, our pets mean everything to us and do, literally, become members of the family. What about them? For some, it might not be terribly heart-wrenching to ask a friend or brother to take care of your dog after you die, but for others (and I would venture to say the vast majority) your concern for their wellbeing is as great as it would be for a child. After all, our pets have their routines also. And like us, our routines provide a sense of stability.

Most of us assume that we will outlive our pet. But what if we don't? As mentioned in an earlier chapter, you can leave instructions for the care of your pet in your will, but is that your only option?

No.

I have known several people who requested that their pets (especially those who are considered to be of senior or geriatric age) be euthanized in the event of their death, firmly believing that the pet would not do well in another environment or with another caretaker. This is a very legitimate concern. Pets have emotions too.

A friend of mine had two dogs, brother and a sister, who were adopted by their humans together. They ate together, slept together, played together, and guarded the yard together. Then one day, the male simply dropped, the likely victim of some kind of heart failure. After being buried in the backyard, the female stopped eating or drinking. She stood over the grave, stared at the ground, and simply waited. For days. It was heartbreaking. After the fourth day, her humans made the decision and she be euthanized, and then buried with her brother. Can pets die of a broken heart? I honestly think they can.

I've seen pets do that with their humans too. Even if they're being cared for by their new owners, it's just not the same. I've known several people ask if their pet can be euthanized after their death. In some cases, if the pet is an older one or needs some type of ongoing and often expensive medical care, a veterinarian will acquiesce.

Legally, you can be appointed a guardian over a person, but the term 'ownership' is used for animals. In other words, in the legal world, your pet is your property, such as a television, vehicle, or your pots and pans. If you die before making arrangements for your pet's care, they will literally become the property of the state.

As of this moment, federal law considers pets the same way they consider other forms of property. Legal arguments from animal rights groups and others are constantly challenging this wording or classification.

So what rights do you have to make decisions about your pet in the event that you die?

Considering pet euthanasia?

This is a difficult topic, I know, but it must be considered or at least included in this section regarding document organization. You will need to have at least some ideas or documents already completed that provide for your pet in the event that you die. In certain situations, you have another option.

It is not unheard of, especially when it comes to older animals or those in declining health, that a family veterinarian would take pity on the situation and understand the stress that a pet undergoes following their (human) owner's death. After all, quality of life for pets is just as important as for people.

While some animals would make the transition, especially if they're younger, every situation is unique. Euthanasia is not a comfortable topic for many. The word is derived from the Greek '*eu*' that implies goodness and '*thanatos*', which means death. So, euthanasia is often called the 'good death' as it implies a death without suffering.

Just the thought of leaving a beloved pet behind, to be at the mercy of strangers – who are simply not *you* – is very difficult for some. I've known several older pet owners who made the difficult decision to have their pets euthanized and then buried with them in a cemetery after they passed on. Morbid? Or compassionate? I'll leave that up to you.

How does this process work when it comes to a beloved pet? There are a growing number of services that perform euthanasia services in home-based scenarios, in a setting that is more comforting to both the pet and their human. First, your pet is given a sedative and analgesic pain medication that encourages sleep. After ensuring that the pet is deeply asleep and doesn't respond to stimulation, the final injection is given.

The fear that many pet owners have, especially if they are aware of their own decline, is that even after making arrangements for pet care following their death, there are worries that the new pet owners will change their minds. This is especially true when dogs or cats don't take to their new owners and can become very different than they were prior to the owner's death.

Like people, pets go through grieving periods. They may become standoffish, fearful, and maybe even aggressive. Unfortunately, there are times when such pets are surrendered to a local Animal Humane Society. This, too, is a horrifying thought to pet owners who want only the best for their pets after they pass on.

The practice of home euthanasia has grown in popularity over the past decade. These services are primarily performed by veterinarians or licensed professionals who have established their own pet euthanasia services. Such professionals are available in every state. Services also have access to crematories and offer a variety of after-cremation options for pet owners such as dispersal of ashes or containers.

Veterinarians around the country realize that the cost of care for an elderly or otherwise terminally ill pet can be beyond the financial means of the owner or a person who inherits the pet following its owner's death. I will say quite plainly, however, that the idea of euthanizing a young dog will come with a few challenges when you consider approaching a veterinarian or an at-home pet euthanizing service. Your pet's condition, age, any disabilities, and so forth will be carefully considered. In some cases, the idea of euthanizing a younger cat or dog is only made in the event that it becomes violent, unmanageable, or vicious.

Re-homing a pet is always going to be the first suggestion made. Yet I have known situations when a pet left behind has been re-homed several times, which makes for poor quality of life for that pet.

Making the decision is not easy, but it is an *option*, especially for older pets who, just like people, may have a hard time acclimating and adjusting to new circumstances or homes.

Pet ownership or guardianship?

As mentioned, the topic of pet ownership or guardianship is a tough one, as is the decision to euthanize a pet based on its age. The point is to confer and consult with a close family member or friend who takes your considerations and concerns as seriously as you do. This is a big decision, and must not be entered into lightly. For this reason, in your will or living trust, it is recommended that you designate a new *owner* for your pet.

When considering the potential need to give your pet into the care of someone else, always make formal and legal arrangements. Don't simply rely on a verbal promise. After all, things change. People move away or grow apart. Have a legal document created that provides for the ongoing homing and care for your beloved pet, along with monies set aside that you can bequest in order to help pay for the care of your pet. You can also find additional information at the Dogs Trust website at dogstrust.org.uk.

Importance of pet ownership written in a will or a pet trust

If you designate a specific person to become the owner of your pet and that is mentioned in your living trust or will, that person will receive any money left to them to help them care for your pet. That said, the new pet owner *is not under any obligation (legally)* to use that money for the care of your pet. However, if you choose someone that you trust to do the right thing, this is at least one burden taken from your shoulders when it comes to making your final wishes.

In addition, when you make provisions for your pet in a will, none of those provisions will take effect until you die. However, if you set up a *pet trust*, you can make any and all provisions you want, and can have some peace of mind in the event that you become incapacitated or unable to care for your pet due to unforeseen circumstances that are not going to lead to death.

Note: When bequeathing ownership of a pet to someone else, always include, in a separate document, instructions regarding the pet's care, habits, and routines.

So what's the difference between the designation of ownership in a will or a pet trust? In a pet trust, the new pet owner or trustee will also receive the pet *and* the money. Under a pet trust, the trustee *must* follow instructions for the care of your pet, and the money *can only be used for the care of your pet.*

That said, be aware that pet trusts will end automatically when the animal dies, and are not designed to continue ad infinitum, such as in the event that the bequeathed dog or cat has kittens or puppies. The trust does not apply to the kittens or puppies, only the bequeathed dog or cat.

When it comes to leaving an amount of money for the care of your pet, always consider his or her age and overall physical condition. Caregiving instructions in a pet trust must be very detailed, and it is important to discuss these instructions more than once with the potential adoptive pet parent. This can include day-to-day habits, times when they need to be let out to go to the toilet, when they're fed, what they're fed, treats, toys, and their sleeping arrangements. You can be as detailed as you want. After all, your pet has their own quality of life issues as well.

Details are important. If your dog is used to sleeping on the bed with you and your new prospective pet caregiver doesn't allow that, there are going to be some issues. After all, the point of providing a pet trust is to ensure that your pet has *continuity of care* and, as much as possible, a similar living environment as well as habits that were previously enjoyed.

Another benefit of initiating a pet trust is that it can kick into action if, for some reason, you become sick or incapacitated and unable to care for your pet. The person that you designated as your pet caregiver can take custody or oversee to the care of the pet during this time.

Conclusion

Whether it's minor children or dependents, a pet or another animal, it's important to think about and make plans for those worst-case scenarios and seek legal advice to determine the laws of your state.

Rest in Peace, not Pieces
A 10-Step End-of-Life Planner

Step 9: Arrangement for Loved Ones Left Behind

Task	In Progress	Done	Location
Explore guardianship options for loved ones if applicable			
Discuss guardianship with family or friends if applicable			
Maintain forward momentum on end-of-life planning			
Designate durable power of attorney and medical power of attorney if not done so			
Make a decision regarding any pets or pet care, including ownership			

Additional notes

....
....
....
....
....
....
....
....
....
....
....
....
....
....
....
....
....
....
....
....
....

Planner pages available to download here

> Have nothing in your house that you do not know to be useful, or believe to be beautiful
> – William Morris

Step 10:
Photographic Memories & Keepsakes

When was the last time you took stock of all those photos, the letters, the newspaper cuttings, the recipes, and other stuff? I covered some of this in Step 8, but those photographs and other mementos require a bit more consideration and care than simply deciding which piece of furniture stays or goes.

You might think that your photographs are organized. After all, a lot of them are in photo albums, right? Chances are that you haven't reviewed them in a while, and you may be surprised to open that photo album to find that the sticky stuff is no longer holding half of those photos in place, or they've come out of those little corners that you used to tuck photos into scrapbooks.

It's up to you to know what to salvage and what to let go.

I knew a woman who lugged around two large boxes of old photographs of the family dating back a few generations. She knew that those photos had meant a lot to her parents, so she was very diligent about becoming the 'keeper of the photos'. Over time and several moves, however, she began having second thoughts. Not only were the boxes heavy, but they took up a lot of room.

Finally, one day, she sat down to organize them. Starting with the first box, she went through the photos. She was the oldest daughter and knew the most about the family history. The first thing she did was get rid of any picture that didn't have a person in it. Then she went back through the stack of photos that had pictures of people. If she didn't recognize who was in the photo, it was doubtful that anyone else in the family would either. Who's going to remember the third cousin from the maternal side of the family in a photo that was taken in the 1950s or 1960s?

When she narrowed down the photos, she realized she only had a shoebox of photos – the most important ones. Much more manageable – and meaningful. Even so, when she started going through her things, she asked the family members if they wanted the old photos, most of which were in black and white. No one seemed interested. Disappointing, yes. But it's important to be prepared for such decisions.

It's all about pacing

When it comes to organizing your photos of keepsakes and the memories they trigger, whether it's a photograph, a newspaper cutting, or letters, pace yourself. It's impossible to do it all at once. In fact, set the timer for one or two hours to start. It's not just a matter of organizing the photographs that takes the time. It's the time spent tripping down memory lane. When you stop to remember a specific event, a location or place or person in a photograph, it's easy to get lost in your memories. One memory might lead to another and before you know it, an entire hour has gone by.

Expect a couple of time warps as you proceed. Some of those memories will bring a smile while others might bring tears. You must gird your loins for an occasional roller coaster ride of emotions. Because of this, it's also important to find a comfortable place to organize your photographs. Kneeling next to the box on the garage floor isn't going to cut it.

Another step that might make the job easier, is to organize your photographs into separate categories. Of course, this may take up some room, so a dining room table or a corner of the living room floor might give you the space you need.

Photo albums are often a logical place to start. Some may be in better shape than others. Some bulky albums will be falling apart by the time you get around to them, and the photographs found inside may not be in the greatest condition, especially as age has a tendency to yellow photographs.

In other words, don't be surprised if all your precious memories are not in pristine condition, especially if it's been a while since you got those albums or storage bins or even cardboard boxes out of your closet, basement or attic. Be prepared to let some go.

Your first step when going through photographs is to not really look at the photographs per se, but their condition. If they've been damaged due to mold, extreme yellowing, or even cracking or bubbling, it's best to put them in the 'bin' pile.

After your first look through an album or section of a box at a time, you may consider (if they're not already) organizing them by year. This may be a little more challenging when it comes to old family photos, especially those sepia-colored ones from the early 1900s. Some people have family photographs dating back into the late 19th century as well. Salvaging them will depend on condition.

If you're like many of us, you may have boxes filled with a variety of photos of different people, places, and events of life

– and not in any particular order. In that case, it might be best to make a plan. How?

Decide how you want to organize the photos. As mentioned, choosing categories for your photos might make the job a little easier. For example, you can organize the photos and put them in separate piles based on:

- Decade (if you can determine) – or years (child, teen, adult)
- Location (such as a first home, a vacation)
- Family photos versus acquaintances' photos
- Children and/or pets

If you're fortunate enough to come across photographs that someone actually bothered to date and identify, that can make the job of categorizing much easier.

If you decide to go the category route, create stacks. You can do this one box at a time or one album at a time. Then, go through each stack and decide what you want to keep and what you're willing to let go.

All those negatives!

If you're like many of us that actually used film cameras before digital cameras and iPhones came along, you're likely to have quite a collection of negative filmstrips that accompany either photographs in separate envelopes, or willy-nilly all over the place in between the photos. It can be quite time-consuming to hold those negatives up to the light to see what might be on them, so many people opt to simply toss them. After all, where do you take negatives anymore?

Actually, the good news is, you can take your negatives to many places that have film developing and processing capabilities, including retail and drug stores that still have photo centers, like some CVS and Walmart locations. In fact, they can typically provide a printed photo from the negative or scan the photos into a digital format. However, keep in mind that these are shipped off to third-party photo labs, as most locations have ceased the development of film in-house as of 2022.

Other options for negatives are also available, including major companies like Kodak. Kodak offers what is called a Kodak digitizing box. Professional photographers are also an option. A number of businesses today, like Kodak, will accept your negatives and can either create prints or digital prints that can be stored on a CD, a flash drive, or stored in the cloud, depending on your preferences. Many of these locations are also excellent in the restoration of old, faded, or somewhat damaged photographs.

Deciding what to keep and what to throw away

It's hard to get rid of old photos, even if you haven't seen them in years. After all, you captured a moment of time and it may be hard to let it go. Even so, expect a percentage of your photographs to not be worth keeping. For example, remember those photographs where your eyes turned red, or even more horrifying, white? What about those double exposures, or those pictures where eyes are closed or the image is blurry?

And the duplicates! Back in the day, a free set of duplicates was actually a perk to save money when getting your camera film printed, and you may find that half of your photos have duplicates. Good chance that you can get rid of those.

The same holds true if you can't identify who's in the picture. Again, if you don't remember, chances are that no one else will either. There might even be pictures of people you don't care for anymore, or those images with scenic shots that you can't even place.

Go with your gut. After all, is your son or grandson really going to care about that picture you took in the middle of the New Mexico desert at that cool gas station where they sold the first beef jerky you ever tasted? Or that picture of an elk up in the mountains that you have to squint to find against the backdrop of the trees?

Don't hesitate to ask family members or friends to also go through the 'throw-away' stack you've kept and ask if they recall anything about those events or the people in them. If they don't, you might want to go through that stack again and cull it even more. If they do remember, try to put some kind of date or explanation/location on the back of the print.

Remember that your overall goal of going through old photographs is to reduce the amount of stuff that your loved ones may have to go through. It's worth repeating that the burden of guilt in doing so may lay heavily on their shoulders. After all, having to go through decades of photographs of you in happier times may be extremely painful for them, not to mention the fact that they may not have the room to hang onto them, nor much of a desire to because they don't know half the people in them.

Reassure your loved ones about your photographs. Let them know if they want to keep some they can, but if they don't, that's all right too. You hung onto them over the years because you wanted them. It's the same thing as we discussed in Step 8 about organizing your stuff. What has mattered to you all these years may not mean the same thing to them. It's not like they consider it junk, but if they don't mean anything to sons or daughters, nieces or nephews, or even cousins, there's no point in expecting someone to hang onto them forever.

Digitizing photos

With the massive popularity of iPhones today, most people now take photos with their phones and store them on those phones forever. I've known people with thousands of photos on their iPhones. Not one of them has gone back to the very first photo they ever took with their phone. Amazing, right?

However, if you want to hang on to some old photos, you can have them digitized. There are a number of businesses that specialize in transforming your most beloved photos or images onto flash drives or even store them in the cloud for you. When you contact a business to do that for you, they will often send you a box that you put the photographs in and then send it off. In a week or two, you get back a flash drive with all the images stored on it. Otherwise, you can spend hours and hours scanning and downloading photos to your computer.

About old letters

What about all those old love letters that you've kept in that shoe box up in the attic? I know a woman who kept all the letters that she and her then boyfriend sent back and forth from the time they met in junior high school. Then, after he went into the Army, she saved all those letters back and forth too. They got married. In the end, there were hundreds of letters, cards, and postcards. She didn't really want to let them all go, but she didn't really want her family reading through her private correspondence either. She ended up keeping only a few and letting go of the rest (she used a shredder).

Like photographs, those old letters can be scanned and digitized. However, chances are that old love letters or even yearly birthday or anniversary cards are rarely looked at. Save the ones that are special and then make a decision about letting go of the rest.

Other keepsakes

Do you have a stack (or two or three) of old newspapers in your garage? You know, from back in the day went people got most of their news from newspapers? Most of us of a certain age might remember more of those famous headlines and articles than others, including but not limited to:

- The King is Dead (the day Elvis Presley died)
- Dewey Defeats Truman!
- Beatle John Lennon Slain
- Nixon Resigns
- Kennedy Killed By Sniper in Dallas
- Princess Diana Dead

While some of these newspapers might very well be worth something to collectors, unless they were carefully preserved, they may not be worth trying to sell or even salvage. The same goes for *Life* magazines, *Saturday Evening Post* magazines (especially the covers painted by Norman Rockwell), some *Sports Illustrated* covers, and even your old comic book collection (depending on topic and condition).

The same holds true for any collection of vinyl records, dolls, stamps, and coins. Coins and stamps might hold some value, but it depends on how many of them you have, how well they were stored, and what kind of condition they're in. Rare coins are always of interest to numismatists or coin collectors, but it all depends.

However, that said, it is estimated that over 60 million philatelists (stamp collectors) can still be found worldwide. Whether stamps are in mint condition, postmarked, or still in their original sheets, it might be worthwhile looking into selling them if no one else in the family shows an interest.

Baseball cards are not as popular with the younger generations as they used to be, but collectors are always on the lookout for that special baseball card. However, as with any collection, items must be in relatively good condition. Proper storage, reducing exposure to the elements or the effects of dust, humidity, or dry heat, can have a huge impact on the value of anything.

In most cases, unless something is in mint to very good condition, collectors are not going to be interested. Of course, there's always auction websites like eBay to consider, but sometimes, those can also be more trouble than they're worth, especially when it comes to packaging and shipping.

Other keepsakes such as spoon collections, or a particular item that you tried to pick up from every state you visited (such as a coffee mug, keychains, or refrigerator magnets) may have been a lot of fun for you, but won't mean much to those left behind, unless one or two evoke special memories of their own.

That said, if you do have a collection that you feel might be worth something, make a few phone calls and find out. Today, professional appraisers are easy to find online. In most cases all you have to do is send or upload a photograph and offer some information regarding description to the site. Be aware that these kinds of services can cost a few bucks (generally $10-$30 or so). Some may require a monthly membership to enable a search of average pricing for what you have.

If you feel that something you have hung on to for years (or decades) may be worth some money, it's recommended that you get a professional appraisal or opinion from a certified appraiser. These can be found by contacting the American Society of Appraisers or the Appraisers Association of America. For an appraisal of this sort, you'll get a fully detailed written report regarding current value. They will also provide you with information on how that item was appraised. Costs for this kind of service are either charged on an hourly or a flat rate basis. For this kind of work, be prepared to spend an average of $300 an hour, depending on expertise and experience.

Note: When getting an item appraised, avoid those who charge a percentage of the item's value!

It is also suggested that you get an appraisal of an item before you take it to your neighborhood antique store, where there is often a lack of expertise and of course, the store will want to make a profit on anything they sell, so you may not get as much for it as you might expect.

Another good source for finding appraisers is to contact an estate attorney or collectibles dealer. Collectible dealers should be certified by national appraisal boards as well as have a good reputation. You can read online reviews if available.

Another way to estimate value of any antique or collectible, you can visit the reference section of your local library or order a copy of a recent antiques and collectible price guides. Most of these offer hundreds of categories and can include but are not limited to:

- The Standard Catalog of Baseball Cards
- The Guidebook of United States Coins
- Beckett Almanac of Baseball Cards and Collectibles

- Scott Standard Postage Stamp Catalog

Again, it's hard to go through your photographs and other keepsakes, only to realize that you've hung onto them for years or even decades and there is very little interest in them from other family members. Some of us collect the oddest things, and depending on generation or even year, these things can change constantly.

So, it doesn't really matter whether you've collected movie posters, records, or even dolls or toys or lunchboxes or tiny Hot Wheel cars, or even first additions or signed books. Get them appraised.

Of course, if you have a family member that has shown interest in your collections, as mentioned previously, you can bequeath that collection to them in your will, even if you stipulate up front that you don't know if that collection is even worth anything. Sometimes, it's not just about the money or the value of something that's important to a surviving family member or friend.

People collect the darndest things, and like they say, one man's junk is another man's treasure. So, you just don't know.

Your ultimate goal is to make it easier on your loved ones or friends when it comes time to go through your things. The more you can do now to make it easier on them later, the better.

As you go through this process, make a list of things that you think one family member or friend might be interested in and ask them if they want you to put it aside in a box they can pick up later. It doesn't matter if it's photographs, an oddball magazine or two, a couple of old records, or whatever. If you think of someone who might even have an inkling of interest in it, go ahead and ask. No pressure, no obligations. A simple yes or no will suffice.

Organizing letters, photos, newspaper cuttings, or other collectibles is one of the most time consuming processes in organizing your life and tidying things up a little bit. But doing so will make it much easier for those you leave behind.

Rest in Peace, not Pieces
A 10-Step End-of-Life Planner

Step 10: Photographic Memories & Keepsakes

Task	In Progress	Done	Location
Organize photographs			
Assess collectables			
Digitize photos if desired			
Go through old letters, cards, and magazines			
Contact appraisers if applicable			

Additional notes

....
....
....
....
....
....
....
....
....
....
....
....
....
....
....
....
....
....
....

Planner pages available to download here

> **Death smiles at us all;**
> **all we can do is smile back**
> **– Marcus Aurelius**

It's A Wrap!

Whether you read this book through from cover to cover before you even get started putting your affairs in order, or you've taken it step by step, I hope that it has provided some beneficial information about how to make progress now, rather than waiting.

This is a huge, often daunting task that is filled with emotion and maybe even some doubts. Even if *you're* ready to get started, family members may not be. They may think you're being morbid or depressing, but really, it's neither.

At the other end of the spectrum, it's hard to put yourself in the frame of mind where you are ready to talk about a subject which is, quite frankly, pretty much taboo in a lot of families. Unfortunately, what happens when you don't deal with this ahead of time is that family members are left literally to pick up the pieces of your life. Isn't it better that you do as much of it as you can by yourself?

I know so many people, friends, family, and simple acquaintances, who absolutely refuse to start this conversation with their parents. It's scary. It's heartbreaking, but it's something that should be encouraged. It doesn't even have to be about death and dying. You can simply encourage downsizing, or making a living space easier to get around in, especially as we or our loved ones age.

However, it *is* a sensitive topic for many, and it's not just your own emotions that need to be dealt with, but those of children, siblings, parents or grandchildren. While you may want to be more organized before it's time for you to leave, others may not want to think about you leaving at all.

Be prepared for comments like, 'Why are you doing that now? Do you know something I don't?' Or 'Why are you getting rid of all your stuff? Doesn't it mean anything to you anymore?'

Whether you're nearing retirement age or you're well past it, there are always benefits to organizing your life. Don't put off making some arrangements or at least *starting* on a plan of attack when it comes to your final wishes, no matter how tempting. We always think that there's going to be a tomorrow and sometimes there just isn't.

I fully realize that talking about death and dying is an uncomfortable topic for many, but it's also a necessary one. Your ultimate goal is to reduce stress, not only on yourself, but on your family members at that moment in life where things are going to be tough enough as it is.

Besides, isn't it always important to communicate your desires and your expectations with family and friends? Don't you want them to know how to take care of the business or the stuff you leave behind? And remember, where there's a 'will', there's a way, and those wills, power of attorney documents, and insurance policies are going to be very important for those you leave behind.

My own experience with my mother made me realize just how important this process is. It can be especially difficult for a person experiencing the earlier or middle stages of any form of dementia, not to mention the strain on their loved ones. The things that surround us provide comfort and memories. Yet, as difficult as it may be to admit, many of those favorite things that mom used to treasure are not even recognized anymore, as far as what they mean, where they got them, or when.

There is nothing more heartbreaking than going through family photographs with a family member with dementia who has trouble remembering their own face when they were younger, or that of a brother or parent. It can also be extremely frustrating for them to try as hard as they might to remember the name of a person that they recognize but don't know how that person fit into their lives. However, that isn't true of everyone.

I know someone whose husband was diagnosed with vascular dementia. As things became more difficult for him, his wife had family photos such as those of his parents, himself when he was younger, and his own siblings printed up in 8 x 10 photos. She put them on one wall of the living room. During the earlier stages, when she still had to be at work, she made sure that he could call her if he got confused and didn't know where he was, or thought he was in someone else's house. She would tell him, *'Go to the wall with the photographs. Do you see the picture of your father? Your mother?'* This was a way to reorient him and let him know that he was in his own home, in his own living room, and that he was safe.

Of course, as time went on, while he may not have remembered who was in those pictures, he knew that they belonged in *his* house, in *his* living room. It brings tears to my eyes just to remember those times, and many of us are going through those difficult stages of a loved one's life already.

The key is to prepare! You cannot prepare too much or too soon. You never know what tomorrow may bring. Wouldn't you feel better knowing that you've made a good effort at estate planning, whether you have a lot or a little to leave behind? The same thing goes for how you want to leave this world. Why make your loved ones guess or worry that they might have made the wrong decision?

It's always important, for people of any age, to maintain adequate medical records and information, especially advanced directives in case the worst happens when you least expect it.

No, there really is no good time to talk about death and dying, whether it's to your parents or your children or other family members, but it is necessary. What if you didn't do any of this organizing? Can you imagine the uncertainty, the confusion, and the roiling emotions that your loved ones will have to go through when there's no plan, no structure, and no organization?

Disagreements and maybe even arguments may crop up. Resentments can lead to estrangement. Some family members are already so busy with their own lives, that it would be difficult to carve out enough time to take care of end-of-life matters. Sometimes there's no one to share those burdens with.

Small steps can make the entire process much easier, not only on yourself, but your loved ones. Do you *really* want to leave a mess for them to take care of? Of course not.

Having your life organized ensures that your wishes will be as respected as much as possible, even though you risk putting some family members through what is known as anticipatory grief. This is normal too, as a part of the grieving process, and is common in those who are family members of one diagnosed with a terminal illness, including dementia.

Besides, when you get rid of excess clutter, you're able to appreciate your most cherished or valuable items even more.

Don't wait until it's even more difficult, emotionally, and physically, to organize your life, when you're hampered by ageing limitations. Don't leave it to your children or your younger family members, because it's a burden on their own lives when they're trying to work, maintain their homes, or raise a family.

If you follow these 10 steps to organizing your life before you die, you will feel much better when it's all done. While you might get some pushback in the beginning from family members, in the end, they'll feel better too.

I hope you enjoyed reading *Rest in Peace, not Pieces: A 10-Step End-of-Life Planner* and found the contents useful. As with many things these days, reviews are important for success and very often determine whether someone buys a book or not. I would be hugely grateful, therefore, if you could spare a moment to leave a review through your Amazon account. Thank you!

Planner pages available to download here

References

Lustbader, R. 2023 *Wills and Estate Planning Study*. caring.com. Retrieved August 1, 2023, from https://www.caring.com/caregivers/estate-planning/wills-survey/

HM Government. *Intestacy – Who inherits if someone dies without a will?* Retrieved October 14, 2023, from https://www.gov.uk/inherits-someone-dies-without-will

Citizen's Advice (2023, November 6). *Who can inherit if there is no will – the rules of intestacy.* https://www.citizensadvice.org.uk/family/death-and-wills/who-can-inherit-if-there-is-no-will-the-rules-of-intestacy/

DRN Law. *Who is responsible for debt after death?* Retrieved October 14, 2023, from https://www.drnlaw.co.uk/what-happens-to-debt-when-you-die/

HM Government (2023, November 6). *Tell Us Once.* https://assets.publishing.service.gov.uk/government/uploads/system/uploads/attachment_data/file/1180365/tell-us-once-easy-read.pdf

EQ – Death Notification Service (2023, November 6). *Death Notification Service.* https://www.deathnotificationservice.co.uk/

HM Government. *Lasting Power of Attorney.* Retrieved October 14, 2023, from https://assets.publishing.service.gov.uk/government/uploads/system/uploads/attachment_data/file/211171/LPA114_health_and_welfare_LPA.pdf

Apple. *How to request access to a deceased family member's Apple Account.* Retrieved August 1, 2023, from https://support.apple.com/en-us/HT208510

HM Government. *War Pension and Armed Forces Compensation Schemes Complaints Process Change.* Ministry of Defence. Retrieved October 14, 2023, from https://www.gov.uk/government/organisations/veterans-uk

NHS. *Advanced Decision to Refuse Treatment.* Retrieved October 14, 2023, from https://www.nhs.uk/conditions/end-of-life-care/planning-ahead/advance-decision-to-refuse-treatment/

HM Government. *Lasting Power of Attorney Duties.* Retrieved October 14, 2023, from https://www.gov.uk/lasting-power-attorney-duties

Organ Donor. *Organ donation.* Retrieved August 1, 2023, from organdonor.gov

NHS. *Organ Donation.* Retrieved October 14, 2023, from https://www.organdonation.nhs.uk/

American Society for the Prevention of Cruelty to Animals. Pet planning information. Retrieved August 1, 2023, from https://www.aspca.org/pet-care/pet-planning

Legal Wills. *Can I include my pet in my will?* Retrieved October 14, 2023, from https://www.legalwills.co.uk/blog/pet-trust

HM Government. *Applying for Probate.* Retrieved October 14, 2023, from https://www.gov.uk/applying-for-probate?step-by-step-nav=4f1fe77d-f43b-4581-baf9-e2600e2a2b7a

HM Government. *Trusts and Taxes.* Retrieved October 14, 2023, from www.gov.uk/trusts-taxes

The Law Society. *Trusts.* Retrieved October 14, 2023, from https://www.lawsociety.org.uk/public/for-public-visitors/common-legal-issues/trusts

Estates or Trusts. What is a Revocable Trust? Retrieved October 14, 2023, from https://www.estatesortrusts.co.uk/differences-between-revocable-and-irrevocable-trusts.html

Citizens Advice. *Arranging a Funeral.* Retrieved October 14, 2023, from https://www.citizensadvice.org.uk/family/death-and-wills/arranging-a-funeral/

HM Government. *Making a Will.* Retrieved October 14, 2023, from https://www.gov.uk/make-will

Expatica. *A Guide to planning wills and estates in the UK*. Retrieved October 14, 2023, from https://www.expatica.com/uk/finance/money-management/wills-in-the-uk-465433/

Cremation Association of North America. *All Things Cremation*. Retrieved October 14, 2023, from https://www.cremationassociation.org/search/default.asp

National Institutes of Health. *Getting Your Affairs in Order: Advanced Care Planning*. Retrieved August 1, 2023, from https://www.nia.nih.gov/health/infographics/getting-your-affairs-order-advance-care-planning

American Association of Retired Persons. *Free Advance Directives Forms by State from AARP*. Retrieved August 1, 2023, from https://www.aarp.org/caregiving/financial-legal/free-printable-advance-directives/

Vehicles for Veterans. *How to donate a car, truck, RV, boat, or motorcycle*. Retrieved August 1, 2023, from https://www.vehiclesforveterans.org/car-donation-form/

DOJ. *Guardianship*. Retrieved August 1, 2023, from https://www.justice.gov/elderjustice/guardianship

HM Government. *Becoming a special guardian*. Retrieved October 14, 2023, from https://www.gov.uk/apply-special-guardian/who-can-apply

American Society of Appraisers. Retrieved 2023 from https://www.appraisers.org

Made in United States
Orlando, FL
01 April 2024

45359110R00085